Marianne Brindley

Western Coloured Township

Problems of an Urban Slum

with photographs by
RODNEY BARNETT

Ravan Press
Johannesburg

Published by Ravan Press (Pty) Ltd.,
P.O. Box 31134, Braamfontein, South Africa, 2017

First printed 1976
ISBN 0 86975 049 6

Printed by Creda Press (Pty) Ltd.,
19 Bree Street, Cape Town
Bound by Edward D. Seabrook,
19 Bree Street, Cape Town

Contents

Chapter 1
Background to the Study

Western Township is eight kilometres west of the centre of Johannesburg and is zoned for Coloured occupation only. It covers an area of approximately 75,7 hectares, with 2 000 dwellings accommodating an officially estimated 12 000 people.[1] Four-fifths of the area is characterised by small two- to three-roomed sub-standard houses averaging 13 m^2 per room. Approximately one-fifth of the people live in the row-houses and flats of the redeveloped part of the Township called Westbury. This study is primarily focused on the old area, which is notorious for its underdevelopment, alcoholism, insecurity, poverty, violence and sense of vacuity: it has every appearance of a slum.

Few adults of either area have an education higher than Standard 8. Most of them are employed in skilled, semi-skilled, administrative or clerical work.

Origins

The origins of the Coloured people[2] lie in the miscegenation of early white settlers, Hottentot slaves and the African inhabitants of South Africa. In Johannesburg the Coloured population is young (the mean age in the old area of Western Township is 23,7 years) and consists not only of traditional 'Cape Coloureds', Malays and others who have migrated to the city from various rural areas and towns, but also the offspring of unions between black,[3] white and Coloured people of Johannesburg and the Reef. Their language is a hybrid Afrikaans or English. Their way of life and social position reflect an ambivalence between white and black society: descendants may be heirs of both and accepted by neither.

Aim and Method

This study deals with the dominant trends in thinking and behaviour which characterise life in Western Township. The area was recommended by the Johannesburg Coloured and Asian Affairs Department as being a problem area noted for its sub-standard living.

The research has an ecological framework in that it views the community, its institutions and patterns of life as an inter-connected whole, and relates this system to the wider ecosystems in which the individual operates. I have sought to portray life in the Township accurately in the hope that we may come to recognise and rectify the difficulties besetting its inhabitants.

The information in this study was obtained by means of depth or open-ended interviewing and observation in people's homes amidst the daily routine. Interviews were either tape-recorded or the main points noted during discussion and written up immediately afterwards. Seventy-five people were interviewed in this manner and 12 additional families were investigated intensively. No interview was refused and I was conscious of playing a neutral, objective role in the area.

A catholicity in choice of family was made possible at first by Health Visitors' recommendations as to 'good' or 'bad' families, and later through personal observation of the environment and consideration of various focal groups in the area: thus alcoholics, parents of gangsters, unemployed or disabled people, grandparents, unmarried mothers and fathers and also children were interviewed. Interviews were conducted either in Afrikaans or English or both, as desired by the informant (most Coloured people speak both). A questionnaire was initially formulated to obtain information on the family setting and this was applied to a 4,2% sample of Western Township mothers.[4]

Although the Township is burdened by suspicion and strain, I received little hostility as a white researcher. I think this was because:

(a) I worked independently and had a genuine interest in the people's way of life and how this affected their children; *(b)* people are sensitive to sincerity; *(c)* Western Township has had no scientific research carried out on it before; and *(d)* the people were pleased to be noticed.

I rarely managed to interview for a whole day at a time; emotional exhaustion was the daily legacy of four hours in the Township.

The Character of Western

Throughout the week in Western one can see ragged and somewhat inhibited yet playful children, young men in gangs lounging at street corners or playing dice, alcoholics heading for some or other destination, men out of work, or women washing the family clothes in tubs of water in the backyards.

During winter the smoke settles thickly in the gaps between the tiny houses, each of which has a small bare yard with outside faucet and toilet. Inside, the homes are invariably cramped and dark, with the occasional religious tract or calendar adorning the walls. Rarely does a floor have a carpet on it: sometimes a piece of linoleum, often just concrete. But the homes are swept and cleaned daily. Unless people build on, the houses are two-roomed, the one room usually containing a table, sofa or chairs, kitchenette and coal stove; the other, either the parents' bed or as many beds as can be fitted in. There is rarely much food to be seen apart from a few essentials.

Breakfast is invariably a meal of left-overs, white bread or porridge; lunch consists of porridge or bread with gravy, jam or soup; and supper, rice with curry, porridge with gravy, or for the few, meat, potatoes, and vegetables cooked with garlic. Because many in the community are religious, Friday is frequently fish day.

Throughout the week Western is a township very much involved in the routine difficulty of living in a poor environment. On Sundays, however, children dress in bright pinks, yellows and reds, adults put on clean clothes, and there are jellies and custards and instant-puddings for lunch. Apart from the most socially disorganised homes where Friday's pay packet has already evaporated in drink, Sunday is a day of gaiety, visiting and comparative leisure. There is a respite, however brief, from some of the more acute problems besetting this harassed and needy people.

FOOTNOTES

1. According to the population figures published by the Department of Statistics in 1974 there are 2 306 000 Coloured people in South Africa: 9,3% of the country's population. (*Population Census 1970: Families,* Report No. 02-03-01, Pretoria, Government Printer.)
2. This is the current official designation for this group of people.
3. Black is here used to refer to all population groups not officially classified as white, i.e. Africans, Asians, Coloureds.
4. This investigation preceded the present independent study. Preliminary reading and the nutritional survey lasted for one year, depth investigation a further six months. The socio-nutritional statistical results are lodged with the Department of Haematology, South African Institute for Medical Research, Johannesburg.

Chapter 2
Birth, Birth-control and Babyhood

Family Size
Traditionally the Coloured people have had large families: 'Ten is the ideal number of children for me, but today it's too expensive.' For practical reasons mothers like having many children: 'Two children fight a lot; more don't.' 'If you have a lot of children you find they are less selfish than if you have just one or two.' 'Big families have a close relationship. They are not selfish. They share the little they have.' But despite the fact that many mothers feel that familial relations are sounder and the child develops a more favourable personality in a larger family setting, mothers are beginning to think in terms of fewer children. The random sample[1] of the whole area indicates that three to four children are desired by most mothers because they feel they cannot otherwise cope with the cost of living. (The average number of children born to mothers is four to five.) Depth interviewing endorsed this finding. A mother who desires two to three children explains: *''n Mens kan nie bekostig om baie kinders te hê. Jy kan hulle nie gee wat hulle nodig het as hulle te veel is.'* ('A person can't afford to have lots of children. You can't give them what they need if they are too many.'), or: *'Die tyd is sleg. Alles is duur.'* ('The time is bad. Everything is expensive.')[2]

Over 50% of women said they would like at least 'a pigeon and a pair'[3] – a son and a daughter – often for psychosocial reasons in that there is a close identification linked with feelings of status and fulfilment between a mother and her daughters and a father and his sons: 'Two girls and two boys – that's nice when you go out – the father walks with the two boys, the mother walks with the two girls.'

The clearest example of the trend away from having larger families was concentrated in a group of women crouching around a coal fire at 08h30 on a cold winter's morning whilst drinking and passing around a carton of 'Bantu Beer'. They all felt that 'a boy and a girl is enough these days' and laughed hugely and mockingly about 'that *slum-vrou* ("slum-woman") in Western. Do you know, she's got 13 children! *Sy gaan nie werk nie, want sy het mos haar eie babie fektrie!*' ('She does not go to work because after all she's got her own baby factory!')

Spacing
Ninety per cent of the Coloured women interviewed in the random sample found spacing a meaningful concept and favoured two to three years between children, which accords with the actual figures. Their reasons are practical and focus on both mother and child. 'I like two years between babies. By that time they eat, they walk, they're off my hands – they can say a few words.' Another who favours three years expresses it this way: 'It gives the mother a chance to rest from pregnancy. The child is big enough to help itself.' *'Twee jaar is meer gesond vir die vrou. 'n Mens word siek en swak van kinders kry agter mekaar.'* ('Two years is healthier for the woman. A person becomes sick and weak from having children close on one another.') 'With two years in between I can cope better, or else you do not look after the child properly.'

Attitudes towards Contraception
The statistical study of the area reveals a dichotomy between awareness and use of three of the most important contraceptives, as seen in the following table:

Method	*Percentage aware of Contraception*	*Percentage using Contraception*
Pill	91	8
IUD	62	4
Injection	74	8

The gap between knowledge and practice, coupled with the mothers' clear acceptance of the **principle** of smaller families was blatant both statistically and in depth interviewing. What emerges most clearly is *(a)* that women are terrified of the allegedly negative side-effects of the contraceptives promoted by the Family Planning Clinic in the Township,[4] even though the population in other respects values European medicine; and *(b)* that **most women do not understand what the words 'birth control', 'contraception' and 'family planning' mean in either English or Afrikaans.**

There is widespread belief that the Pill produces cancer, illness, headaches and nausea. Some feel it makes you thin. One woman in a group of Christian mothers whose husbands were teachers, said: 'A doctor told me, many women have died from the Pill,' another: 'A doctor at Coronation Hospital[5] said women have got brain haemorrhages from the Pill.' 'The Pill blocked the tubes of another lady; I won't use it' – this woman has two children and finds them tiresome. There is also the belief that if two 'brands' of the Pill do not suit you, then 'the Pill is no good for you'. Some people say 'because you get the Pill from the Clinic it is 25 cents and it is R3 from the Chemist; the Clinic does not give you such a good Pill'.

Moreso than the Pill, there is a definite belief that the Loop 'makes people thin'; the Loop is also commonly suspected of producing cancer in women. One woman inquired about the Injection as she was thinking of having it. She was not interested in the Pill and certainly not in the Loop. A friend of hers was on the latter: 'The Loop tore her insides and pus came out and she got cancer from it and was terribly sick.' Many women have heard of 'the pains you get from it'. Others express dislike because 'women have had babies from the Loop'.

The Injection does not engender as much spontaneous criticism as the foregoing methods, but women do tire of having to go to the Clinic every three months for it to be repeated. It is disliked because it makes women 'too fat'. Women quite frequently said they were not given the Injection because their blood pressure was too high.

Some women try one or other method of birth-control and feel it fails them. They tend to lose heart and give up. One mother used the Pill but did not feel well on it, nor on the Injection, and she fears the Loop. Now she does not use any form of contraceptive although 'three children are enough; I can't manage to bring up more. But if it happens, it happens.'

Another typical statement is: 'I have seen people sick from the Pill and Injection. I would rather bring a child into the world than make myself ill with birth-control.'

There is thus a whole corpus of women who desire smaller families but who are not prepared to risk their health in the process.

Other women feel safer using their own form of contraceptive. '*Ek drink baie koue water, twee koppies vol, net van die kraan uit voor ek gaan slaap*' ('I drink a lot of cold water, two mugs full, straight from the garden tap just before I go to bed.') This is quite a common method. Another is to swallow a mixture of lukewarm water with *Entressdruppels*[6] (which is also said to be effective in delaying menstrual periods).

Apart from fears to their health, religious convictions are a prominent factor militating against contraception. A number of women prefer to leave the whole problem of family planning to God.

'Ek het nie die voel daarvoor nie. As die Here wil hê dat ek 'n baba kry dan sal ek dit kry, as nie dan nie' ('I don't have the feeling for it. If God wishes that I should have a child then I'll have one; if not, I won't.') This commonly-made statement links up with the fervently held religious belief of the Coloured community at large. 'A child is a gift from God. If it comes it comes, and you must accept it – but I'm not yearning for a child.' Fairly typical is the mother of six whose children all sleep in one bed in a bare two-roomed little house. She has severe marital problems: her husband drinks, beats her regularly and gives her only R1–R2 a week for food. She is not interested in birth-control and will tell you with suddenly sparkling eyes: *'Die Here is groot. Hy sal sien wat ek moet kry.'* ('God is great. He will see what I must have.')

This abdication of personal responsibility in favour of God is consistent with the intense religious belief of most Coloured adults. Taking into account that they do not yet have political viability as a people, that their lives are beset with poor health, marital disruption, alcoholism and illegitimacy, that there is very little trust between male and female and that the South African situation to a large extent denies the adult the opportunity to have some say in his own destiny, one is led to believe that it is their personal uncertainty that leads them into a fatalism which would rather leave the whole problematical matter of living to God who in his wisdom will give to them according to their needs.

South African politicians and leaders of all racial groups in this country constantly maintain that the reason why the Coloured (and African) people resist family planning is because they regard it as a device used by the present Government to reduce their populations and thus enhance the security of the whites.

Apart from a few educated, more intellectually or politically aware people I found no support for this supposition on a conscious level in Western Township although as mentioned above (with regard to religious considerations) I do believe that political factors in this country are **subconsciously** a deterrent to effective family planning. It is not that there is a one-to-one correlation between apartheid and the reluctance to use contraceptives but that the **effect** of apartheid is an important determinant in the Coloured person's loss of confidence in his ability to make positive decisions for himself, and in sustaining the interest and energy to do so.

Some women feel it is natural for a woman to bear children and one should not interfere with the processes of nature. 'I'm quite satisfied. I've had three years between all my children so that's O K . . . after all I am a woman.'

One shebeen owner is symptomatic of the more tradition-bound sections of the populace. She has a 12 year old son hovering on the fringes of gang-life, two children living with her husband's mother, two with her own mother, two with her at home and one still being carried on her back in the manner of black mothers. 'I won't take any of that birth-control. In the old days and in my mother's days women didn't take all those things and they were much stronger than they are today. They didn't get all these headaches, stomach cramps and sicknesses that these people who are using the Pill and those things are getting. My mother had ten children and it did her no harm but these women who are having two or three children, they aren't strong.' Other women feel that they like to be free, but 'with Family Planning you are not free'. These will not use any form of birth-control at all.

Many women are pressurised by their husbands not to use any contraceptive device. Such men tend to want children only for personal prestige. One husband gives his wife R2 a week for groceries and nothing for his four children's clothes or schooling either during the year or at Christmas, but spends most of his time drinking. He calls his children 'dogs' when drunk and beats them, and when sober declares: 'I didn't ask to have a bath full of children!' The mother was using the Pill but he took her tablets away. She says of him: 'He want to give children, but he can't support.' In the old area of the Township women are not infrequently heard saying of such husbands: 'He always wants the children when they're big but he doesn't treat them well when they're small – he just shouts.' Another mother says she refuses her husband's sexual advances because she is 'afraid of babies. As soon as I'm pregnant he doesn't care any longer and he doesn't want to support them. But I suffer to bring them up.' Many men for financial or psychological reasons are unable to manifest responsible family behaviour.

On the other hand there are men who fear that their wives may be unfaithful and therefore refuse to allow them to use a contraceptive. Yet when a female resident suggested that men should have to share the hazards of contraception and also take a Pill, the women were vociferously divided because 'a husband would just go off with other women – you can't trust men'.

The Role of the Family Planning Clinic

There is thus a need for the Family Planning Clinic *(a)* to pay greater heed to the psychocultural factors influencing the **male** and *(b)* to establish a skilled counselling service in such a community, whose staff can sensitively detect the needs of the individual in relation to his husband or wife and children and develop people's trust in one another. Trust particularly needs re-affirmation because of the nature of contraception itself which has obliterated the safeguard of pregnancy in proving unfaithfulness.

Finally a number of mothers boycott the Family Planning Clinic because if they attend with an infant under two years of age and it is thin they are criticised for child-neglect: 'and I'm not going there to be moaned at.' Mothers say they are given little real choice of contraceptives, that they are treated coarsely and 'like children' at the Clinic, and others find they cannot 'waste a morning and leave the other children at home'.

Most were unaware of the need to have PAP smears or their Loop checked periodically. Others were not prepared 'to waste time' on the matter, or could not find someone to care for their other children regularly while they went to the Clinic.

It is imperative if family planning is to succeed as a concept, that the service offered is as comprehensive, humane and protective as possible or else those people who are motivated to plan their parenthood but have no alternative source of medical care such as private doctors, will refuse to co-operate with any such programme and will thus adversely affect the thinking of other women in the community.

An increasing number of pediatricians are finding that mothers only begin to accept family planning when their children survive, and their morbidity and mortality rates are reduced.[7] (Wallace and Gold, 1972, p. 8) A successful family planning programme must have as a priority improved health services for children and nutritional support programmes for the mother.

It follows that **only when people receive real social security in the form of good wages, incentives, status and personal opportunities, will their need to find security and meaning in children be minimised.**

Thus although in the present generation of adults one can excuse ignorance of birth-control and fears concerning it, we must ensure that these mothers' children not only have education to improve their standard and grasp of living, but that they receive meaningful counsel in family planning, health, and responsible marriage.

Only then will mothers begin to be guided more by intellect and reason rather than by mythical belief with no foundation in medical fact.

Terminating Pregnancies

Although abortions are at present illegal in South Africa,[8] home-made abortions are a viable clandestine form of birth-control in the Township. The best methods of obtaining an abortion are held to be that the woman drinks one of the following: *Wonderkroonessens,*[9] paw-paw pips mixed with water, washing blue mixed with soot and water, or 'Essence of Life'.[10] A more painful but common method is to put cotton-wool on a stick, cover it with glycerine and then pierce the uterus via the vagina.

One lady was visited by her 36 year old friend who performed an abortion in her outside toilet. 'I've never seen a thing like that in my life before. I didn't know it was so bad – oh, did she suffer! But she's O K now and today she's gone to work. Don't tell her mother, will you? She would throw her out of the house.' Often of course septicaemia results, though some women say they prevent this by drinking *Wonderkroonessens* as it has a cleansing effect.

In general, public opinion within the area maintains that abortions are reckless and wrong behaviour. One mother verbalised this: 'These women who are having the abortions are hating the child for the father and then you don't want the child, but it's not the child's fault.' Others feel that if a woman is having problems with her boyfriend or husband then abortions are condonable. Many mothers admit that life is too difficult, that they are broken by marriage or the inability to rear decent children in such an environment and feel that if they fall pregnant again they will have no conscience in aborting.

Less frequently there are babies who are killed after birth because the mother can't cope. This is also illegal; public opinion whilst not really opposing home-made abortions, condemns infanticide. One of the worst deaths mentioned was of an infant, newly-born, found suffocated with sand pushed down its throat. Such women are often referred to as 'nice-time girls'; frequently they are associated with the belief that 'they won't get children when they marry . . . people just kill children these days.'

Satisfaction with Contraception

Although only a few women are satisfied with contraception, reference to their attitude is important as a future ideal for the community. One devoted mother of eight who has been sterilised is utterly relieved at not being able to bear more children, although since the operation she maintains that she has lost interest in sexual intercourse. Before that time she used to say to herself: '*Kyk daardie vroumens se kind is al groot, ek verwag alweer. Ek het al moedeloos geword; dan dink ek, maar my man is maar so goed vir my, dis sy kinders wat ek groot maak, waarom wil ek dan baklei; dit maak nie sense nie.*' ('Look, that woman's child is already grown-up, and I am expecting again. I had already become despondent; but then I thought: my husband is so good to me, they are his children I am rearing, why do I want to fight, it doesn't make sense.') She often recalls how she used to remain heartsore when other women looked younger and were healthier with only two or three children. Finally, after the birth of their last child the husband took the initiative and said: '*Nee ons moet 'n plan maak, ons moet 'n dokter gaan vra, want ons kan onsself nie beheer nie.*' ('No, we must make a plan, we must go and ask a doctor, because we can't control ourselves.')

She somehow manages to clothe, wash and feed all her eight children in a tiny two-roomed house on R70 a month, and feels that times are hard now, but she is grateful that her struggle to make ends meet will not be increased by additional children.

Thus the picture of planned parenthood in Western Township is rather bleak and requires greater two-way communication and co-operation between the Health Visitor and the community.

Conception

Although all the women interviewed were aware that coitus causes pregnancy, there are various personal theories about the actual mechanics of consummation.

One is that if the woman experiences her orgasm at the identical moment to her husband, then 'that's it!' and she's pregnant.

A quasi-religious explanation put forward by a woman who had been the eldest of 17 siblings, is that conception 'is part of Nature. It is when you quarrel that you get pregnant. You have been going, say two weeks after your period and you fall out with your husband, then you have sex together – you will have a baby, because that is Nature's way of making a family again. But in the end it's God who decides. Because God is the Creator, isn't he, and if he doesn't want you to have a baby you won't, and if he is pleased that you will have a baby, you will.'

A different theory concerns itself with a person's premarital history, maintaining that this affects a woman's rate of reproduction and ability to reproduce. *'As jy eenmal rondgeloop het met ander mans en jy het pregnant geword dan is dit in jou bloed en jy sal al die tyd 'n kind kry.'* ('Once you have played around with other men and become pregnant, then it is in your blood and you will conceive more readily.')

Perhaps because illegitimacy is common in the community the illegitimate child is treated sympathetically by most women, though the professed ideal is for the mother to bear a child in marriage.

Miscarriages

Quite a number of women have miscarriages as a result of violent marital quarrels, with husbands chasing or beating wives. Such wives often speak of falls resulting from jumping out of windows to escape. Many women treat the resulting haemorrhage themselves, either by drinking a compound of herbs or by mixing a cinnamon stick with crushed garlic and vinegar and cooking these in water. When the mixture appears brown it is drunk.

Pregnancy Beliefs

During pregnancy many women take liquid paraffin or Milk of Magnesia daily 'to clean the stomach' and if they feel weak they take *Versterkdruppels* (strengthening drops)[11].

A number of women feel 'it is horrible to be pregnant because of the cravings'. Some of these cravings have little after-effect to their way of thinking, as in the case of the woman who while pregnant ate half a kilogram of apricot jam a day, or another who only ate fruit and drank Coca-Cola, whilst another had the overpowering urge to drink ash. (Coloured women will drink ash mixed with water as a folk remedy for blown tummies or heartburn – as do a number of African people in connection with religious beliefs – sago ash has also been found used in places like New Guinea for nutritional purposes. (Townsend et al, 1973, p. 93 and 96)

It is further believed that certain negative patterns of behaviour or excesses will influence the foetus' later characteristics if they go unchecked. *'Ek dans baie met swanger en daarom spring my seun baie en loop rond.'* ('I danced a lot when pregnant and that is why my son is so active.') Or 'I had a craving for fish and sardines when I was pregnant. That's why my boy is drinking like a fish today!' (Her adult son is an alcoholic.)

Less light-heartedly, anger receives attention in two ways: some women maintain that if you are very cross when pregnant your child will be malformed; others that a woman must not become angry during gestation otherwise she will produce an irritable and bad-tempered child.

A number of people believe that if you stare at or insult an ugly or bad person when pregnant, your child will resemble that person. Those who hold these views do not however believe that a child inherits all of a mother's personality traits – only her negative behaviour. It is also thought that if you see a crippled person and laugh at him or her when you are pregnant you will bear a crippled child, and if you hate certain people your child will resemble the person you hate.

The encouraging aspect of these pregnancy beliefs is that they are child-centred, and already in the foetus stage serve to condition the expectant mother into conducting herself in a way that will benefit the infant. Thus when the time of parturition arrives the need for the mother to centre most of her activities around the new infant is only an extension of an already established behaviour pattern. Furthermore the moral pressures against antisocial behaviour symbolise an attempt made by the culture firstly to encourage people to tolerate those whom one might not like, and secondly to explain the existence of people with negative characteristics. It is hoped that by the correct ritual action undesirable traits will be minimised in the new generation. Physiologically speaking to advocate equanimity in the expectant mother is of course a sound principle promoting positive character formation of the foetus in the womb.

The culture also manipulates certain food values inductively, testifying to both the risk entailed by the birth process and the precautions mothers should take to ensure their own safety – thus eggs should not be eaten by pregnant women because they are said to prolong labour. Such customs re-emphasise the closeness and importance of the mother-child bond, for '*as jy te veel eiers eet wanneer jy swanger is dan kry jou kinders eier koppe net soos daardie onder in die straat.*' ('If you eat too many eggs when you are pregnant then your children will have egg-heads just like those down the road.') Similarly some Coloured women will not eat mangoes or paw-paws when pregnant lest the newly-born infant should be subjected to yellow-jaundice.

It is interesting to note that in other areas of the world like Tamilnad (South India) paw-paw avoidance during gestation is symbolically linked to various human conditions such as feminine discharge. (Eichinger Ferro-Luzzi, 1974, p. 12) Similar beliefs are held by certain Melanesian Islanders: 'The banana, the mango, the malay apple, the South Sea almond, the paw-paw, the breadfruit . . . are forbidden to her [the pregnant woman]. This taboo has reference to the future health of the child.' (Malinowski, 1968, p. 192)

Birth

Despite the availability of the adjacent Coloured hospital, not all Western Township women have their babies delivered there. Some women pay midwives for pregnancy and delivery visits, though others for a variety of reasons still give birth at home to at least one baby and feel confident in doing so. Many of them state that Coloured women are unafraid of birth pains because '*ons Kleurling vrouens ons weet hoe om te relax.*' ('We Coloured women know how to relax.') They find the nurses at the hospital 'with the modern methods keep ordering us about and they tell you to press at the wrong time . . . and then the baby goes up and down and you lose time.'

Some women drink Cane Spirits to aid delivery; others drink Gin when about to give birth because it eases the process 'even though you feel sick the next day'. Not all use alcohol as an aid however. Others mix a raw egg with lots of pepper and eat it, for as they say, this helps dispel the afterbirth early.

A number of women who give birth at home do so entirely unaided except for calling in a neighbour 'to come and suck the moisture from the baby's mouth. One woman had the cheek to charge me R5 for that – when I did it all myself.' Most describe how the day after childbirth they are up and about and wish to clean the house. They recall how bored they get just lying in bed *'en as ek komberse sien wat moet gewas word dan kan ek nie rus totdat ek hulle gewas het'* ('and if I see blankets that need washing then I cannot rest until I have washed them.')

Breast-Feeding

The intimate bond established between mother and child antenatally is stressed again postnatally. Niehoff and Meister (1972, p. 20) reported from a cross-cultural study on breast-feeding that there was a 'widespread belief that a mother could pass personality characteristics to her infant as she suckled him. In Iran it was believed that the mother's milk would influence the morals, traits and habits of her child.' In Western Township, the mothers specialise this belief into the transmission of negative behaviour and in particular, anger.

There is a strong belief in *'kwaai melk'* (bad milk) – that if a lactating mother becomes angry or irritable her child will inherit these characteristics. To avoid such an occurrence, some will tell you that if you happen to have got angry, then before feeding you must first press out a good portion of the breast-milk which would prevent the temper from being passed on to the child. Others say: 'If you are cross your milk can cause a big wind in your child and unless you rub its back nicely it will choke and may die.'

Mothers who believe in this type of interaction with their infant during lactation do not necessarily believe in it during gestation.

The two main sources of advice on infant feeding in the Township are the woman's own mother (31% of the cases) and the Health Clinic (39%).

Qualitative and quantitative questioning revealed that 88% of Coloured mothers favour breast-feeding as opposed to bottle-feeding. *'Bors is gesond. Alles wat ek eet gaan deur die melk. Die melk bly vars. Daar is nie kieme in bors melk. Die kind is nie so sieklik soos wanneer dit op bottel is.'* ('The breast is healthy. All that I eat goes through the milk. The milk stays fresh. There aren't germs in breast-milk. The child is not as sickly as that on the bottle.') 'The bottle isn't real food.' 'The breast gives the best milk for the baby because it is from the mother. It is the cheapest way of feeding – no green diarrhoea as with bottle-babies. You don't have to get up at night to prepare a bottle.' (Coloured mothers in the Township tend to have their infants sleeping beside them in the same bed at night.) Another benefit of breast-feeding is that it soothes the child, especially when it is disquietened. 'The breast is more healthy for the baby's comfort when the child is unwell.' Other mothers maintain that it calms the child while teething though when it begins to bite and makes the nipples raw it is usually weaned.

There is a theory in the Township that the gangsters were not fed on mothers' milk *'want moeders' melk gee jou 'n gevoel vir mense. Hulle moes poeier melk gehad het, want hulle voel niks nie'* ('because mothers' milk gives you a liking for people. They must have had powder milk for they have no feelings.')

The majority of mothers have a sound knowledge of the physical and psychological value of breast-feeding and their point of reference throughout is the child. (Some also mention how breast-feeding provides the mother with a 'nice feeling'.) However

38% of the mothers of the sample had weaned their baby from the breast by the time it was seven months old.

Reasons for Bottle-Feeding

The reason for 53% of the total sample mothers weaning their last-born child off the breast was either because the mother had 'insufficient milk' or '*die kind het van self die bors gelos*'. ('The child left the breast of its own accord.')

Research indicates that lactation failure is a widespread phenomenon throughout the world and although an important causative factor for early weaning may be the enticement of artificial feeds often erronously prepared (Jelliffe, 1972, pp. 199-205) yet it is important to consider the psychosomatic causes of weaning. In this respect Raphael (1973, pp. 121-122) makes five noteworthy points:

(a) Not every woman can breast-feed.
(b) Not all mothers' milk can be tolerated by their infants.
(c) Some women are better lactators than others.
(d) The western way of life places excessive demands on the mother and tends to isolate her from her infant and supportive help. This causes damage to the mother-child tie and leads to lactation failure.
(e) Unless the ejection reflex operates, no milk is released from the breast. 'This sensitive mechanism is very responsive to a woman's emotional state. If the mother is not mothered, the ejection reflex will not function.'

I postulate that for most of the mothers of Western Township their failure to lactate is a consequence of psychosocial strain [*(e)* above]. Tension in everyday relationships and a lack of resistance to the pressures of a materialistic society whose benefits cost too much to enjoy, anxiety, failure to succeed and stress all negatively affect the mother's ecosystem, making the birth of a child something which is not especially joyous.

One young mother of 17 had breast-fed her illegitimate baby for one month and then her milk dried up. It transpired that her mother (who drinks heavily and with whom she has a strained relationship) swore viciously about the baby just before her daughter's lactation failure and then a little later beat her up.

Frequently in casual discussion one hears: 'I had no milk. I suppose it's because I work all the time . . . and I don't have proper meals.' A number of women said that they had much milk until they began to work and then it 'just dried up'.

The need to work was also an important reason for weaning, and the practical problems it poses are common throughout the western world. Reddy (1971, p. 200) provides information on the situation in Jamaica and Barbados, where most mothers (35%) wean their child to accustom it to the bottle in anticipation of their going to work. Even the Coloured Health Visitors of the Township find breast-feeding irreconcilable with a working day. 'At first I used to rush home at lunch hour to feed, but the nanny felt it was upsetting the child as she had no sooner got used to my going than I was back and off again. Also when you come home tired after a day's work you can't just sit down and feed. You have to be relaxed and feel you have time to feed.' (Only a few follow an urban African custom of feeding infants morning and evening and expressing sufficient milk at such times for a lunchtime feed.)[12] Although many mothers are forced to work because their husband's income is insufficient to live on, others say that despite their knowing breast-feeding is healthy for the child, they work because they become restless and bored at home.

There is furthermore a belief in the Township that a woman who takes up employment will be likely to come into contact with dirt. This dirt becomes internalised and if she is breast-feeding will be imparted to the baby through her breast-milk and result in a softening of the fontanelle.

Some women in Western Township hold the belief that expecting another child and breast-feeding are irreconcilable processes. *'Al die mense sê dit is vuil melk, kyk hoe maer word die kind.'* ('All the people say it [breast-milk] is dirty milk: look how thin the child becomes.') Others believe that the **foetus** will be harmed if an elder child is still suckling. A similar belief is found in Senegal where 'weaning during the next pregnancy was sometimes associated with a belief that the milk of a pregnant woman was harmful to her suckling child.' (Niehoff and Meister, 1972, p. 17)

A number of women maintain that doctors at the hospital told them to wean their babies because they were beginning to 'suck blood' and wouldn't in fact be drinking milk any longer. The women say you don't see the blood but the sensation is different. When a baby drinks milk from you the experience is 'slightly painful' as you feel the milk being drawn out, but you 'feel nothing' when the child sucks blood.

Most of the mothers who have this belief do however feel that a child should only be weaned when it is ready for it, for too early weaning would have a detrimental effect on the child's health and composure. Some mothers do not believe in giving their babies milk either from breast or bottle as milk for them is associated with negative qualities especially diarrhoea, the scourge of babyhood. Others believe that after six months breast-milk is of dubious value. One mother weaned her little boy at six months and felt that 'by then he is big enough, I can train him to drink out of a feeding mug . . . If the child feeds on the breast and has teeth they get rotten – sometimes the milk is too rich or else there's no milk and the child sucks blood.'

A few mothers feel shy to breast-feed, and some find it inconvenient: 'If I go to the cinema or anywhere else I can't leave the baby behind if it's on the breast.'

Breast-Feeding as a Measure of Maternal Feeling

Because breast-milk has such outstanding success in preventing protein-calorie malnutrition, it seems right that pediatricians and 'Well-Babies' Clinics should make known its value. At the same time however we should be wary of making moral judgements about a mother who breast-feeds ('good') and one who doesn't ('bad') unless she is one of the few who are careless and negligent: and even then these broad qualitative judgements are misleading.

Although some may concur with the view that: 'The decision to breast-feed is often taken as an index of acceptance of the maternal role' (Bernal and Richards, 1970, p. 251), I believe that the cultural thinking and pressures that women in the society are subject to need to be examined before such an assumption can be made. The Newsons in their Nottingham study (1965, p. 46) found it 'necessary to be extremely cautious in using the duration of breast-feeding as a valid measure of maternal feeling' particularly as in their case, in a modern society with adequate facilities, they found that: 'While breast-feeding seems to be declining at a rate which many will find alarming, the early change to bottle-feeding is combined with a responsiveness to the baby's demands which may make the whole feeding situation more satisfying to him than was the breast-feeding by schedule.' (pp. 60–61)

Women in Western Township feel that a 'good' mother should breast-feed, but modify their thinking since most white women (whose life pattern many emulate) bottle-feed their babies. They also accept the fact that the practicalities of life, such as the need to work or feeling fatigued often take the matter out of their hands.

Weaning

Almost all Coloured women in the Township feel 12 months is the ideal time to wean a child, with the associated belief that the child is now independent, can eat 'proper food' and by then is 'over the tummy trouble'. In short, 'she is big now'. Linked with this idea is a belief that by this time *'die melk is nie meer goed want dit word dun'* ('the milk is no longer good because it becomes thin').

Weaning is regarded as a natural process in the child's growth. Mothers say that if a child is 12 months or more it can understand that one's milk is finished; if it is too young then you rub your nipples with Mixed Masala curry, *Wonderkroonessens* or *Aalwyn* (Aloe)[13] powder and it soon loses interest. Mothers regard as obvious the fact that they will continue to comfort the child whenever necessary after weaning.

Mothers at weaning will either buy pills for drying up their breasts or place brown paper round them or rub them with camphor oil.

Solids

Solid food in the form of cereals or porridge is usually introduced at the age of three months with fruit and vegetables being the second solid introduced at a somewhat later stage. Clinic pressure has virtually eradicated the traditional infants' food of gem-squash, marie-biscuit and milk.

The Caring Mother

The basic concept of motherhood in Western Township is therefore a sound one – it is child-centred and stresses the bond between mother and child from the time of conception.

Although the majority of babies in the Township are not planned for, mothers in general expend energy and care on their children, even if this is often of a summary nature. At the same time it is evident that the mother is severely hampered by circumstances beyond her control in the practical aspect of child-rearing as well as in her own health and energy because she is poor, badly-housed and living in an unsettled environment.

The Problem of Overpopulation

At the 1974 congress of the South African Society of Obstetricians and Gynaecologists, the Secretary for Health in South Africa called for strategies to contain the population explosion. The Coloured people of this country are frequently quoted as having one of the highest population growth rates in the world.

It seems to me that we must approach the matter of overpopulation both on the conscious and subconscious level.

On the **conscious** level many mothers in Western Township desire to reduce the number of children they must care for but are uneasy about the supposed physiological side-effects of contraception. (Similar findings have been made with regard to the majority of American women studied at Parkmed, New York.) Furthermore they are dissatisfied with the attitudes, treatment and aftercare attention they receive at the Clinic. The evidence suggests that family planning experts need to come to terms with people's fears, and that patients' ideas, however odd, must be respected, yet countered compassionately if they lead to unnecessary fear or medically undesirable practices.

In coming to terms with the **subconscious** forces which are working against the desire to limit the size of families, cognisance must be taken of the relevant causes, and the procedures implemented must be based on these. Hseuh et al (1973, p. 99) rightly point out that to date family planning has embodied a **negative** approach by merely advocating fewer children. 'It is this injunction which the family in a less developed country (LDC) finds hard to follow. The LDC parents hope that one or two of their children will live long enough to be able to take care of them in their old age. But in the LDCs infant and childhood mortality rates are very high: recently it was reported (Unicef, 1972) that one out of four children die before the age of five.' Thus parents will for the hope of their own and their children's survival, desire not to limit their offspring.

The more **positive** approach which can presuppose a more positive response is to 'show LDC parents how to have **better**[14] babies, ones which will not only survive but will also develop to their full mental and physical potential, then they would have a powerful and positive argument for overall family limitation.' (Hseuh et al, 1973, p. 99) We need to emphasise the value of a few healthy plants rather than a miasma of struggling emaciated ones.

One of the most important steps that must be taken in this respect is to improve **maternal nutrition.** From Western Township it is clear that mothers urgently require information on an adequate protein diet and supplementation during gestation and lactation. Researchers have found that underfeeding of rat dams during these critical periods leads to 'poor survival, permanent growth stunting, and delayed achievement in physical performance of the progeny'. (Hseuh et al, 1973, p. 104)

It is imperative that a Health Clinic offering both preventive and curative medicine be available at least for all pre-school children up to seven years when the child is physically vulnerable, especially in places such as Western Township, where apart from the one hospital children after the age of two have no medical care.[15] Furthermore such facilities must establish a reputation of caring, efficiency and good human relations.

In this context the socio-economic position of the Coloured people must be improved, for until their social security as adults individually and collectively is assured, they have no alternatives in life nor any reasonable incentives to lessen the number of children they bear. For it is at present children which give them pleasure, status, comfort and a sense of achievement. The rising cost of living per se is too crude an incentive to be the sole motive for such communities to curb their population growth.

Provision must also be made for the Coloured people to experience a political identity, that first of all they may know who they are and to which respected group or community they belong. Housing programmes must be revised. People in the old part of Western Township are weary and resentful of bringing up their children year after year in overcrowded shells of houses without any modern facilities such as electricity, baths or hot water. Too many children are left at home without adequate care because the mother finds 'I have to go and work to get bread for my children'. The environment is depressive and children are on the street. Meaningful education is necessary. Adequate pensions, adequate pay and a secure job are preconditions of assuring people that they can rely on the State for whom they work, rather than on one of their many children for support.

The above areas of concern are I believe the most important blocks to effective family planning amongst the Coloured people of Western Township in particular. But the basic principles involved apply to most countries, namely, that **until people are given real meaning individually and collectively, and have an identity as well as security in society, they will seek to find these primarily in their offspring.** Governments and the Medical Profession must be prepared to come to terms sympathetically and realistically with the subconscious forces which motivate communities. Although the cost of social security programmes will be great, it will be less than that involved in large scale population expansion and the concomitant ills that will accompany it.

FOOTNOTES

1. This refers to the statistical results of investigating one mother in every hundred households; as against the more personal, informal and multifaceted depth interview data.
2. I have left the Afrikaans as it is spoken, even where ungrammatical.

3. A corruption of the English saying: 'a pigeon pair'.
4. The Family Planning and 'Well-Babies' Clinic are housed in the same building in the Township and are staffed by two separate sets of Coloured and white nursing sisters from the Johannesburg City Health Department.
5. The 547 bed hospital adjacent to the Township serves the Coloured population of Johannesburg (approx. 90 000 people).
6. One of the Lennon's brand of medicines popular in the area and recommended for stomach-ache and heartburn.
7. In this regard it is worth noting that the infant mortality rate for the area is unacceptably high: 55,7 per 1 000 Coloured infants. Compare this with the figures published by the Department of Statistics for the rest of the country: whites 20,9 and Asians 35,6 for every thousand infants in 1971. (1974 Bulletin of Statistics, June, Table 1. 2.)
8. *The Abortion and Sterilisation Bill,* February 1975, states that abortions are illegal unless two medical practitioners certify in writing that the pregnancy endangers the life or physical or mental health of the woman; or that there is a serious risk that the child will be born irreparably physically or mentally defective; or where the foetus is the product of unlawful intercourse such as rape, incest, or contravention of the Immorality Act; or if the woman is an idiot or imbecile.
9. A Lennon's brand of medicine used before birth or if a woman has menstrual troubles.
10. A compound of aloes, alcohol, ginger, rhubarb, gentian, myrrh, galangal, cucumber, sugar, treacle and water. It is used for menstrual pains and as a post-natal cleanser.
11. Another Lennon's medicine: this serves as a tonic.
12. This milk is bottled and then given to the infant by the 'doula', or mother-substitute.
13. Commonly used to clean the blood and for stomach-ache.
14. My emphasis.
15. The comparative study of Mindlin and Lobach (1971, p. 430) in a slum and middle-class neighbourhood of New York indicates that the most successful method of organisation is to offer both curative and preventive care in the *same* setting, otherwise mothers tend to place a lower value on preventive medicine, especially after the age of one.

Chapter 3
Folk-medicines for Young Children

There is a body of women scattered about the Township who know and use folk-medicines as well as European medicines. Few of them have the luxury of going to a private General Practitioner and many will if possible use some home-device before going to the Out-patients section of the hospital.

European Medicines

The Lennon's brand of old Dutch medicines is embedded in the home remedies of the area. If infants can't sleep, for instance, Lennon's *Rooilavental* is mixed with milk to act as a tonic (this is also used for babies or anyone feeling 'uncomfy inside' or having cramps or heart-trouble).

Young infants are kept healthy by rubbing one drop of warmed *Stuipdruppels* or *Versterkdruppels* over the child's body. *Groenamara* is used for stomach-aches, *Versterkdruppels* for headaches or heart-pain, and if the mother feels low she takes a mixture of all the brands together.

Mothers are quite experimental in this regard. Some have successfully applied Colgate Toothpaste for burns, also Calamine lotion, others say an excellent remedy for drawing out phlegm from a bad cough is to smear Vicks on Sunlight Soap wrapping paper and place this on the chest. The paper will then draw out the phlegm.

Folk-medicines

Garlic and green ginger feature extensively in both the community's medicine and cooking. Garlic and ginger with water are swallowed for stomach pains, asthma, and babies' coughs and colds: 'It drives them up and out.' Garlic is also smeared on the child's head to prevent it contracting a cold, though neckbands and armbands may also be worn by young children for this purpose. Green ginger cooked with half an Anadin or Panado and water, or with a little Lennon's *Rooipoeier* (Red Powder) serves the same purpose. For sore throats a gargle is made with Red Powder or an aspirin mixed with water.

Some people find relief from 'being short of breath' or 'suffering heart trouble' if they boil a little thyme in water. Others cook a beetroot and eat it when it is still hot to provide relief from piles. One woman is an inveterate snuff-taker and uses a small tin a day. She finds it clears her head and helps her to think, '*maar dis die beste vir my senuwees*' ('but it's the best for my nerves.')

In other cases, a castor-oil leaf is placed on the head or stomach of the child (or adult) to draw out pain. Some heat the leaf and place it on a flannel to use as a poultice. One mother rubs all her infants with castor-oil on the temples, forehead, palms of the hand and soles of the feet to keep the '*vuiligheid*' (dirt) away, and she swears by it as a protection against gastro-enteritis. She no longer administers castor-oil internally because 'the new castor-oil is not as good as the old': it makes the child too weak by overworking the stomach.

I once brought a mother a geranium plant. She was delighted, for she now could apply its leaf to a tooth for toothache or place it in her ear when she has earache.

Mothers also say that a raw egg sprinkled with brown sugar and placed on the roof for a night (or day, depending on the theory) is a most effective cure for whooping cough. For measles *'vlieg tee'*[1] is highly recommended.

The range of folk-medicine in Western is extensive.[2] One still meets the occasional inexperienced mother with listless children whose youngest cannot sleep, is allergic to milk and repeatedly suffers from malnutrition, until the worn-out mother feels 'the child must rather die, I don't know what to do anymore'. But on the whole, in a community which sends out so many patent signals of distress and helplessness, it is encouraging to see mothers actively caring for their children and trying to cure their illnesses. Even though the folk remedy may in some cases amount to nothing more than superstition, it serves the function of giving to those who impart it a sense of achievement. It aids people in their will to live and strengthens their feeling of confidence in their ability to overcome adversity. Health Visitors need to sift out which cultural cures are medically harmful or ineffective and to suggest alternatives to these whilst tolerating the others. It is important not to scorn those who are trying to help themselves.

Protective Magic

Side by side with European adaptive and folk-medicine there is evidence of protective magic in the Township. A number of mothers will place garlic, cloves, camphor, *Duiwelsdrek, Entressdruppels, Doepa,*[3] dry mustard and *Haarlemensis*[4] (in various combinations) in a little bag and hang this on the neck of the eldest son or daughter for its first six to nine months of life, basically to protect the child from becoming polluted and weakened by others. '*Hy sal nie die geestelike goete kry en al die vuiligheid van baie mense . . . Hy dra dit . . . en as dit losraak en dit raak weg – moenie soek daarna nie. Glad nie! . . . Ons glo nie daarin nie maar om troubles te avoid . . .*' (He won't catch the spirit things and all the dirt of many people . . . He wears it . . . and if it falls off and is lost – don't look for it. Not at all! [for it is polluted now] . . . We don't believe in it except to avoid troubles . . .')

Misused Medicines

One young mother who had been unhappily reared by foster-parents has a little boy of 16 months. She complained that he had a 'running-tummy' for three weeks but it stopped for the first time the day before I visited her. She laughingly exclaimed: 'two weeks ago he ate a whole bottle of Eno's. He loves Eno's . . . Then last week he ate a whole packet of icing sugar . . . He also loves Aspirins and unless you hide them he would eat the whole bottle! And Dispirins he loves – I often give him a quarter or half of one because he likes them so much.'

Worms

There is a common belief that the frequent occurrence of worms in children of the area is the result of them eating white bread or mielie meal every day – nevertheless the majority of people still continue to eat these foods.

Teeth

The cultural incentive in Western Township is towards an absence of natural teeth. Adults prize having a full set of upper and lower dentures, preferably with a gold or silver tooth in the front of the mouth as status symbols: even though many people admit it is not as easy to chew with false teeth.

The children tend to complain of sore teeth and ask one to pull them out. Generally they have poor and rotten teeth and there is neither preventive nor curative dentistry in the Township. Dental and medical care of this nature must be made available at the important developmental ages of two to seven years. When teeth get too bad, mothers will take the children to the hospital to have them pulled out.

Many Coloured (and African) people feel that Coloureds have bad teeth because 'they eat too much fish'. A number of mothers attribute the cause to the fact that children eat so many sweets and say sweets are especially bad for them when they are cutting teeth. As an example of their affection it is customary for fathers or mothers to give their children one or two cents every day for sweets and there is a constant stream of little children at the local café buying them.

Coming to Terms with Cultural Ideas

The preceding data indicates that the Coloured mother places value on healthy children, although her thinking is permeated with attitudes both medically valid and fallacious.

There is a need when dealing with a heterogeneous population such as this for doctors and all concerned with improving the standard of health **to tolerate those harmless cultural beliefs and attitudes which assist people in establishing roles and defining their value system.** At the same time if a belief or practice is genuinely medically undesirable then there is a need to direct the people's thinking gently towards sounder medical practices.

FOOTNOTES

1. This is properly known as: *Flor Sambuchi.*
2. A similar list can be found for the Zulus in Bryant (1966).
3. *Duiwelsdrek* and *Doepa* are normally used for burns or if children have convulsions.
4. Usually taken for backache or bladder trouble.

Chapter 4
Growth from Childhood to Adulthood

'Personality growth is the result of an interaction between the growing organism and other human beings. In some way the organism assimilates features of its social environment, and in so doing grows increasingly like its culture medium . . .' writes Bowlby in his classic research on maternal deprivation and its effects on the child. ('Maternal Care and Mental Health' 1966, p. 59) In a later abridged and edited edition of Bowlby's work it is observed that 'evidence is overwhelming that an organism – whether human or infra-human – develops through a process of constant interaction with its environment, and that to the extent that its environment is depriving, its development will be retarded or distorted.' (Salter Ainsworth, 1973, p. 223)

In considering the position of the child in Western Township, both as child per se and incipient adult, it is essential to consider the orientations and processes governing the community that are likely to mould him. Because Western is a deprived environment featuring bad housing, sporadic violence and ubiquitous poverty, and because the process of human socialisation is enacted through imitation, participation and play, one is at once led to question whether the child can achieve a measure of human fulfilment here.

Illegitimacy

A child's estimate of his ego is inevitably bound up with the attitudes the people around him hold of themselves and of him and his position in life. In this respect from the moment of birth the Coloured infant is treated with a greater or lesser degree of acceptance depending on whether his skin is light or dark, and his hair straight or frizzy, for these are among the prime criteria of acceptance in the society at large. But the question of legitimacy is also a relevant one.

There is an ambivalent attitude towards legitimacy which in many ways corresponds to the value of the child in the Township. Although amongst the older generation there are Christians who abhor illegitimacy, and one father was so adversely affected because both his late-teen daughters were unmarried yet had children that he claimed to be 'a broken man on account of my children', yet increasingly the popular attitude is amoral and humanistic, indicating a wholesome acceptance and regard for the newly-born child. Many mothers when discussing legitimacy take the stand that it is inconsequential whether a child is illegitimate or not: what is important is *gedrag* or how the child behaves as a person. On this and many matters they are reluctant to pass judgement on their fellows and if they do they preface this with: 'It's not to say that I'm better than anyone else . . .' Consistently then, most people would support the viewpoint of the granny who said: 'Anybody can make a mistake; it's not up to me to punish a woman for this. The Lord will punish if he wants it and the Lord will let live if he wants.' People commonly feel 'anybody can make a mistake'. On a different plane is the position of the woman who has given birth to an illegitimate child. Some regard her with no moral stigma, others feel she has been 'dirtied and it's not nice' for a woman to lose her virginity before marriage. However marriage no longer has as high a standing as it used to have for these people – its failures are too overt.

There is an ambiguity around legitimacy which is both beneficial and injurious to the child. On the one hand the Coloured child does not bear the emotional strain of being stigmatised throughout life on account of being born out of wedlock, but on the other this tolerant attitude, even if born of necessity, leads to the child not receiving the necessary financial support of a father and tends to condone irresponsibility in men who frequently desert mother and children and fail to supply maintenance for their children. In addition to the indigence which illegitimacy often entails, the child also loses a father figure to imitate and lean on.

I believe we have not paid sufficient attention to the findings of psychologists who maintain that for balanced development a child requires **both** sexes as adult models, since they serve different personality functions. The male especially teaches the child his or her sex-role by his masculine attitude and treatment, the female assists particularly in the child's emotional development by a more sensitive empathic relationship. It is held that if either of these is absent the child is subject to some dysfunction: and from this viewpoint illegitimacy and the marginal or absent father warrant our attention.[1]

Bowlby mentions how unmarried fathers are frequently promiscuous and Wittkower (1948, p. 60) links promiscuity with an affectionless, anxiety and resentment arousing environment. In Western Township, in terms of the brittle marital relations, the relatively low wages, the sub-standard living conditions and absence of upliftment, it is understandable that even ordinary fatherhood demands more sacrifice than is often psychologically possible.

As Davis (1966, p. 400) correctly points out: 'The weak link in the family group is the father-child bond. There is no necessary association and no easy [biological] means of identification between these two as there is between mother and child . . . Among human beings a bond is created between the father and his children by a complex set of folkways, mores and laws. The mother's relation to the child is also socially regulated, but in this case the bond is more easily established and maintained.'

It appears therefore that if we wish to make fatherhood worthwhile we must provide the male with the necessary conditions to support his children adequately, so that they can become a source of interest and pride to him instead of an overwhelming financial burden whose pitiful lives fill him with a sense of worthlessness.

The Pre-School Child

The pre-school child in Western is left most of the day to his own devices. A few children fetch picture books from the local library and a few parents tell their children stories or read to them. But in general the child receives no conscious adult stimulation. There is one crèche for 100 children to serve all the pre-schoolers in the Township. There are no play-schools, and although there are two parks and some play-equipment, the parks are not frequently used nor particularly inviting and the swings tend to be wrecked by gangsters.

Almost one-third of the sample children are cared for by domestic servants. Grannies or elder siblings are also involved when the mothers work, and 41% are thus engaged. Invariably this surrogate care lacks the solicitousness that is required for it to be considered a satisfactory arrangement, although there are those who try hard. But even when mothers are at home they are so busy with housework and washing that they neglect the socialisation by activity and stimulation that is vitally necessary for the development of their child. The concept is still foreign to them.

Most of the better-off families, one-fifth of the total, are young and live in the redeveloped area consisting of flats and row-houses. The flat-dwellers constantly complain that they cannot rear children in flats because 'the children have nowhere to play. I keep chasing them out of one room and into the next because they make such a mess and are so noisy.' The same problem has been encountered in sociological studies elsewhere. Jennings (1967, p. 201) found that when British families moved into flats, their vigorous under-fives had nowhere but indoors to play, with the result that several mothers suffered nervous strain trying to keep their children quiet and safe. In Western, as overseas, mothers observe that when their children do go out they overreact and 'are wild'. They are also irritated by the fact that other mothers constantly interfere with their children, who mix or fight with their peers in the passageways of the flats.

Although the pre-schooler is often found helping at home and devising his own pastimes such as flying kites, building mud pies and castles and playing trains with old chairs or hopscotch on bits of carpet, more definite, involved stimulation is needed in the community, especially as the child does not enter school until the late age of six or even seven.

Recommendations regarding Crèches

I should like to see the Government establish more crèches in the Township for children from nine months to two years. It is also desirable that industries receive tax deductions for providing crèches at places of work employing only women, and that steps are taken to establish Play Centres or Adventure Parks for pre-schoolers with the support of the Provincial Administration and local city charities. These could be run by volunteers in the open on a minimal budget capitalising on the ideas of nursery schools throughout the country. It would also help if the Library arranged illustrated weekly 'Storytimes' for pre-schoolers. If a person were centred in the Township (preferably an enthusiastic local inhabitant) she could co-ordinate such activities on various levels, an important element of which would be involvement of mothers, fathers and teenagers. Such worthwhile activities are especially vital in a slum, where efforts at every level should be made to woo the child out of the aimless milieu of the street.

Helping at Home

A distinctive trait of this community is the extent to which children at the pre-school and primary school age have to help in the home. In the early morning one sees them busy polishing floors, sweeping the house, tipping out rubbish, rinsing the evening plates in a basin, and often doing the washing for younger siblings.

Basically the practice of child home-help has a sound origin as one mother who gets her children to help with most of the housework explains: *'Ek moet 'n vrou van jou maak al is jy klein, want ek maak jou vir 'n ander mens groot, jy moet mooi leer . . . en dis waar want wat sal 'n man vir jou sê as jy met hom trou en jy weet nie wat om te doen nie?'* ('I must make a woman of you even though you are small because I am rearing you for another person, you must learn well . . . and that's true. What will a man say to you if you marry him and you don't know what to do?' [ie in the house]).

One feels the child in Western is given responsibility early but there is a danger that by this means parents are ridding themselves of tiresome chores. I not infrequently met seven year old girls doing the family washing because the mother was working, or washing the baby's nappies daily as their job. In one case a negligent mother would not let her eight year old daughter go to school because she had to clean the house and wash while the mother worked.

Children are regularly sent to do little items of shopping for mothers at the local shops. They are also sent to the shops at night for whereas gangsters will kill adults if they are in their way, they usually leave children alone or merely molest and rob them of their money.

Children handle money early: four year olds for instance will borrow money for their mothers from neighbours, though often loans are refused. Sometimes they go shopping with the few cents given them for sweets. In studying 11 local shops for 1½ to 6 hours per sitting children were found to be the most frequent customers. On one Wednesday within four hours I saw a general dealer receive 45 adults, eight teenagers and 225 children making purchases amounting to R28,89: **an average of ten cents a purchase.** The child-customer and low purchasing power of the people are evident. 1 454 people spent R339,23 in 36 hours.[2]

Children are forced to look after themselves when parents work or are drinkers. But even when parents cope with the physical exigencies of life one does not feel they have enough time, energy, or awareness of the psychological needs of the young, or too often they don't know where to look for advice or how best to help themselves. Ignorance to a large degree leads to children going astray.

A shout and a slap at a disobedient child may be an acceptable cultural norm, but what is most disturbing in Western is the prevalence of aggression and physical violence inside as well as outside the homes. Bandura and Walters found 'that children readily imitate the aggressive actions of another person, and that punishing parents may create aggressive children'. (Larsen, 1971, p. 278) I often came across fathers who beat their children for disobedience or swore at and hit them, especially when drunk. The worst case was of a little boy of eight whose writing at school was quite incoherent: his sentences ended in mid-air. One moment he wrote about himself, the next about a city, then about a ball. In confusion an observant teacher reported him to the Headmaster. The facts that emerged were that a month ago this little boy and his brother has seen their drunken father hack their mother to death with an axe.

Survival Strategies

Most inhabitants feel that their children go astray because of the 'bad atmosphere' of the Township, although there are those who manage to ride the turbulent tides of sub-standard living. These people make a conscious effort to counteract the environment. One mother in particular in a mammoth effort of ingenuity has sensitised herself to the environment and decided on methods of combating it for the sake of her children. Her view of the Township and the way she faces it was the most eloquent and positive onslaught on negative conditions that I came across.

Mrs Saunders[3] believes in being firm with children so that they should learn what is 'right' and 'wrong'. Unlike most mothers she does not believe in beating her children for wrongdoing but rather, when they have erred she sits down and discusses with them **why** they have done wrong. She talks to them and does not believe in hiding things as some mothers do; consequently before time she explained to all her children the facts of life, menstruation, the value of work, how to relate to people and behave responsibly and whatever else there is to know or learn.

It is worth noting that when a bus crashed into my car in the Township, it was her eight year old daughter who immediately jumped forward and said: 'Sister, I saw it happen, I will be your witness.'

Mrs Saunders feels frustrated and concerned at the roughness of Western, its degradation, and the negligence of people. Her main problem is that her children, like all the others round about, constantly see distressing things happening – they watch gangsters murder people, ice-cream sellers being robbed, parents hitting and fighting one another, people dumping refuse over the fence into the street; they live with alcoholism and drunkenness, ineffective adults and overcrowding. She knows that all these incidents register in the children's minds; they talk and think constantly of gang activities and the life of the street.

Because she feels the atmosphere of Western affects the thoughts and ideas of her children she tries to devise ways of giving them other things to preoccupy their minds and energies: 'I try to get them away to learn there are other things than what they see here.'

Consequently every year she saves to send her children on holiday to some relative or place where they can be subject to new and more positive experiences. She takes them to the supermarkets and stores to teach them **how** to shop: 'I teach them to be interested in their own shopping basket and not in what other people are taking. They must make a list before they go shopping and buy only what they need and nothing else so they don't overspend.' She or her husband take the children window-shopping in town or to the beautiful Carlton Centre so that they can see exciting things and discuss them together.

Mrs Saunders hates the small houses they have to live in and their lack of privacy, but insists that each of her children must sleep in a bed, so every night they put down the folding divan so that the boys can sleep in one room and the girls in another. She finds the old houses with their lack of facilities 'make your pride disappear', that is why her husband makes a point of painting their house yearly and maintaining a little garden. At night they can't go out because it is too dangerous, so they have bought a gramophone and play music at home or read books and talk.

Her only hope for her children is to distract them from the environment, so she forces them to go to Sunday School even when they don't feel like it: 'At least that's another morning taken up and we must get other things in their heads than this Township.' With the same purpose in mind their father takes them to watch sport on Saturday afternoons and shares the experience with them.

When I visited this household I remarked on the cards on display for the father's birthday. (Birthdays are for the most part uncelebrated amongst Coloured people in the Township.) 'Yes,' she said, 'the children must learn what is the value of a birthday and a wedding anniversary. And now of their own accord they buy these and they make puddings and make that a special day for each person.'

But even Mrs Saunders, who is making such heroic attempts to overcome the poisonous effects of life around her, feels that if they are to be totally successful in their endeavours they must leave Western. 'We want to move to Ladysmith to my home where we have a place. Just as soon as we've saved enough, we'll work there, because you don't know for how many days you will stay alive here.'

This was the most articulate and intelligent mother I met. A similar lady who was well-off financially and resident in the redeveloped area, was sending her son to karate lessons 'for self-defence for this Township' even though he loathes it and would rather take up ballet. This family also tries to go on holiday every year (this is rare in the area) and the mother dresses up as Santa Claus at Christmas 'to give them a nice surprise, but they recognise my hands!' She is dedicated to her children and provides them with as many cultural opportunities as she can afford.

The Hostile Environment

But the majority of mothers do not have the resources to overcome the environment, and they succumb to its forces along with their children. One is acutely aware of the parents' feeling that they are powerless to improve their lot and one of their most piteous pleas was: 'Can't you send my children to a Home somewhere so they can grow up right,' or 'I need a place to cure him [a teenage gangster],' or a request that one might find a school somewhere else so that a mother's children would not turn out to be thieves or criminals. Typical was Mrs Pearson, a mother of nine: 'When my son is ten I must find him a boarding school somewhere because this is no place for a youngster to grow up in.'

The environment is eroding the confidence of parents with regard to child-rearing because they feel the problems are too great. It is essential therefore that the Coloured Affairs Department should stimulate the community into action by means of mutual involvement in the planning, execution and development of Township affairs. It needs to organise relevant adult educational courses, and arrange for a team of social scientists to assist adults and teenagers break the grip of distrust and anti-social behaviour that is destroying life in the area. Under present circumstances one unfortunately cannot turn to the schools to help solve these difficulties for they themselves are fraught with problems.

Schooling Problems

The schools dealing with children from the Township are bedevilled by truancy for one or all of the following reasons:

(*a*) the double-session system makes it difficult to tell which children in the area should be at school;

(*b*) parents don't supervise their children's attendance and homework, or are away at work all day;

(*c*) the content matter of subjects is unrelated to the students' life experiences; and

(*d*) gangsters lure teenage scholars away from school.

Because the one local primary and other neighbouring schools for Coloured children cannot accommodate all the children of schoolgoing age, the position is relieved somewhat by the double-session system whereby one group of students receives morning tuition and another, afternoon. Although there are officials who argue that no school hours need be lost by this system as the overlap time can be used for lessons in the open-air, in practice the teachers maintain that on account of it a child at the local primary school loses six hours of schooling **a week** for its first six years of school, thus falling badly behind. What is certain is that members of the community often do not regard it as their business to know whether children on the streets should be at school or not.

Teachers become further despondent as a result of the apathetic attitude of parents with regard to their children's attendance and achievement at school. They get little response for instance concerning homework supervision. In one class of 40 only five parents were willing to sign and check the work done. They are either not interested or too busy working.

Pollak, reporting on a 1971 education conference which was especially concerned with the needs of Coloured people, states: 'Absence of housing, or living in totally inadequate overcrowded conditions, exercises detrimental influences upon families. Children in such an environment cannot be expected to attain educational standards commensurate with the demands of modern society. Resultant educational problems are a high rate of scholastic retardation, early school-leaving to supplement inadequate family income, poor motivation, and poor performance.' (p. 5)

Recommendations for Improving Schooling

The school curriculum needs to be tailored to suit the type of environment in which the pupils move and think. One of the major setbacks of education in most countries according to Wedge and Prosser has been that the formulators come from a middle-class morality but design courses for students who come from working-class backgrounds. 'Schools tend to be middle-class "institutions" in which most of the pupils are working-class.' (1973, p. 55)[4]

Similarly Clegg describes how in England many varying social pressures in and out of school 'contrive to blunt the main tool of learning'. He quotes a sixth-form student who wrote: 'The problem of speech facing a sixth former in a working-class area is a relatively minor one. It is a reflection of the much greater complexities he faces in having to live two lives, but his speech may be the most prominent manifestation of his embarrassment and discomfort . . . His normal social environment is not conducive to good speech nor to the standard of social etiquette he is expected to acquire . . . Education in general has made him incompatible with working-class life.' (1967, pp. 1–2) The same dichotomy between home and school ideologies arises in Western.

Not only must the Department take significant steps to meet this problem in its planning, but teachers need to be encouraged to adapt their content and method to the pupils' environment so that education will become relevant, meaningful and uplifting. Schooling must equip these children more adequately for employment and the practical realities of life. Courses on Marriage, Planned Parenthood, Budgeting, Income Tax, Hygiene, Road Sense, House Repairs and Alcoholism must be introduced alongside Typing, Accountancy, Woodwork, Metalwork, Home Economics and other conventional skills.

It is imperative that the Department responsible for Coloured education in the Township enforces compulsory attendance at school for **every** child.[5] Each school in the neighbourhood needs to be provided with a Truant Officer who has some training in social welfare to counsel problem children and follow up cases at home, otherwise the flow to gangsterism has no hope of being stemmed. The teaching staff are too frightened of being attacked by unsympathetic parents, quite apart from the gangs.

Only 1,6% of young people aged 13-17 years in the random sample (of the old area) had studied further than Standard 8, though 71% had passed Standard 5. Students drop out of school either because they lose interest (physically mature boys and girls of 14 being in the same class as eight year olds), or because they feel stupid, or because they have to find employment to supplement their parents' income. Some have to care for younger siblings, or do the housework if the mother works, and others feel disillusioned because of limited job opportunities even if they do succeed.

Some parents feel that instead of acting as an antidote, school teachers are condoning violence by being allowed to administer corporal punishment. 'I mean look at my son, he got beaten by the teacher because he came in late from break. The school is not a family anymore. If the children disobey their teachers why don't they separate them, put them in another room or control them? Why must they hit them? The trouble is they don't feel a sense of belonging at school.'

In these respects it is regrettable that the recommendations of the M. C. Botha Coloured Education Commission of 1953-56 have not been implemented in the reality of day-to-day teaching. 'In the case of the Coloured community, the home conditions are often such that the children, to a greater extent than in other communities, lack the educational and elevating influences of a good home, and the task resting on the shoulders of the school is the more important and exacting. For these children – and there is a large number of them – the school can no longer be merely an educational institution in the narrow sense of the word, but must be the pivot on which the general education – intellectual, spiritual, and physical – of the whole child turns.'

The aim of education according to this Commission, must be to create opportunities for the child 'by which his whole being can so develop that he will grow to be a person:

(a) Who will attach the greatest value to, and will strive after, the things in life which will contribute to his own happiness as a responsible, useful, and honourable person;
(b) Who will be prepared to take a part, to the best of his ability, in the service of the community of which he is a member;
(c) Who will take pleasure and find satisfaction in promoting the welfare of his fellow-men, especially those of his own population group.' (Botha, 1953-1956, pp. 5–7)

It is a loss to the children of Western that they are not receiving such an education. We might bear in mind Victor Hugo's observation that 'the opening of a school is the closing of a prison'.

Juvenile Delinquency: Causes and Effects

It is significant that according to the 1970 population census the percentage of Coloured juveniles admitted to penal institutions was greater than that of any other population group in the country. And as shown by Fine (1973, p. 21) offences by Coloured persons aged 7-17 years are primarily directed against property, and secondly 'against life or body'. In the 18-20 age group offences against community life predominate followed by offences against property. Liquor and drugs are often associated with these acts.

As found elsewhere in the world, Coloured **urban** penal convictions in South Africa vastly outnumber those in rural areas. In the United States of America in 1960 larceny and burglaries in urban areas were three times greater than in rural areas, whereas robberies[6] were six times more frequent. (FBI, 1960, p. 33) Similar preponderances of urban vis-a-vis rural offences are reported from European countries such as France, Germany and Holland. Many sociologists feel that the related co-efficients are: the presence of conflicting norms and values, greater individual freedom and anonymity, increased mobility, the importance of materialism, loose-knit networks, and 'achieved' rather than 'ascribed' status. Intimate group participation is inclined to disintegrate and since people are known more casually in a city it is easier to act irresponsibly. Clinard (1964, p. 80) suggests that a lack of community identification is important. 'Poverty and deprivation, prosperity and depressions are important only in terms of the aspirations, needs, socially defined status, and cultural conditionings of the person.' (p. 113) Further, he feels, 'the chief sources of delinquent and criminal behaviour appear to be the general culture, the neighbourhood and associates'. (p. 201)

Bovet in his WHO monograph on juvenile delinquency (1951) emphasises that delinquency is likely to be low 'when times are quiet, community life peaceful, and the standard of living high'. (p. 19) He argues that the origin of delinquency is bio-psycho-social. He believes that the 'psychological common denominator can be found in the feeling of insecurity to which any criminal tendency from whatever source gives rise'. (p. 42) He shows how imperfect adaptation of the ego to the external social world leads to insecurity. 'Whether it is a question of unfavourable social conditions, of financial difficulties, of bad housing, of overcrowding, of harmful and evil companions . . . everywhere is found insecurity born of uncertain material and emotional conditions.' Insecurity gives rise to anxiety and: 'An aggressive reaction is the most usual method of obtaining this relief' (p. 42), which completes the cycle to guilt and anxiety again. Finally, Bovet stresses how traumatically alcoholism in a juvenile's family circle affects the members.

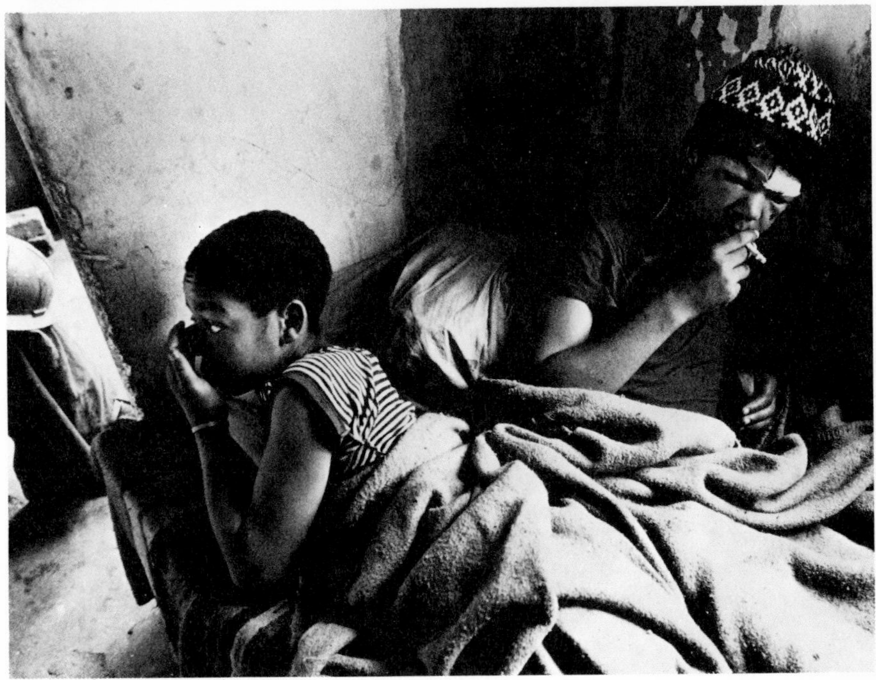

Causes of Delinquency in the Township

All these factors: the rapid social change and individuation, the desire for material symbols, the tension, the high level of gang activity and violence, show why people talk with fear and disapproval of this Township – which they aptly term 'The Wild West'.

The inhabitants hold the following theories of the causes of gangsterism:

(a) Absence of community loyalty and common values

Many adults blame mothers for taking sides with their children when they have erred instead of respecting the judgement of another adult who tries to stop a fight in the street or chastises a child for misconduct. Thus inter-parental conflict becomes rife. 'They just think of their children and no-one else.' These people feel that growing children are allowed to 'get away with' petty, unjust fights and clashes; they are not taught a moral code and no-one's word is ultimately respected.

The situation is analogous to that of the Gómez family, described by Lewis. (1959, p. 75) This is a struggling Mexican working-class home also in the throes of urbanisation, in which the archetype, Rosa, the mother, 'got into quarrels with neighbours because of her children whom she always defended whether they were at fault or not'.

(b) Irresponsibility of parents

Others feel parents act irresponsibly if their child has committed a crime such as rape in the Township. Repeatedly one hears that a white lawyer has been paid R150-R200 by poor parents for the defence of their child (the money is usually borrowed from friends). The gangster is invariably released, returns to his gang, and in two cases known to me has committed the same offence again. 'A lot of the parents spoil their children and feel only for them if they stab someone; they run away to get a lawyer to get him out of trouble; they only feel for themselves, even if their son has done a bad thing. But for me, no, if my son has done something wrong then even if he's my son I will see that he gets punished.'

(c) Neglect by parents

Another cause of gangsterism is '*nalatigheid*', the neglect by parents of their children – because they work, because they don't care, because they have problems of their own, or because they drink. As one man said, 'It's the parents who are fighting together, they have the cocky children.'

(d) Absence of a distinctive male model

Some mothers feel that their husbands have never shown their sons 'how to be a man'; that they set a bad example by their drinking, bad manners and irresponsibility, and in spending wages on themselves rather than their family.

Analagous behaviour has been found amongst other Coloured people in South Africa: *'Ek moet pa én ma wees. My man wil niks te doen hê met die kinders nie. Hy sê dis genoeg as hy geld huis toe bring. Hy praat nooit met hulle nie. Hulle is bang vir hom. As ek oor hulle by hom kla, slaan hy hulle half dood. Ek bly liewer stil.'* ('I must be father **and** mother. My husband wants to have nothing to do with the children. He says it's enough if he brings money home. He never speaks to them. They are scared of him. If I complain about them to him, he beats them half to death. I rather keep quiet.') (Adams, 1974, p. 180)

(e) Poverty
A few of the mothers, gentle, concerned people, feel that their *'armoede'* (poverty) is the cause of their sons now serving two year prison sentences. They haven't enough money to buy even the essentials of food and clothing let alone to satisfy the demands of teenage fashion. Marsden (1973, p. 155) found a similar pattern in England: 'Mothers with delinquent children felt this was partly because the children were dissatisfied with their lot compared with other children.'

(f) Absence of a sense of worth
One mother who tries to be a good mother and whose son is a gangster, verbalised this feeling: 'I think what you are doing in Western is a great thing because no-one cares for Western, and it would be good if the gangsters could feel that somebody does care about them.'

(g) Official indifference to the Coloured people
Some parents feel that the problems in Western Township derive from the fact that: 'The Coloureds are given very little you know . . . what do the children in Western get but wildness? There's wildness in the street, in the bioscope[7] – you can't go and see a film, it's only rubbish and violence and guns and knives.'

The continued inadequacy of the lives of these parents and their offspring, and the frequent absence of real affection and security is aggravated by the fact that there is no manifest attempt by governmental departments to ameliorate their position. Visible meaningful change in the rudimentary structures which overwhelm the morale of the community must be effected **with their approval and involvement.** It must also be realised that every time a person or family is moved from one house to another, be it in the same township or elsewhere, the human dislocation that follows is a heavy psychological price for the occupier and the people around him to pay.

(h) Absence of police protection
Numerous inhabitants are severely critical of the apathy manifested by the local Newlands police towards the crime problem: their inability to break up the gangs; their tardy arrival at fights as a result of the absence of police patrols. The police on their part find that the gangs have become increasingly organised; that the police force is too small to cope with the problem adequately; they themselves are threatened by gangsters, and they feel frustrated by the tendency of assault victims to withdraw their charges (because of further gang intimidation).

(i) Historical presence of gangs
There is a theory[8] attributing the origin of two of the three dominating gangs in the Township to the ardent supporters of the leading local football teams in the 1960's. The Blackpool United fans assumed the name of the 'Fast Guns' derived from the film: 'The Last of the Fast Guns', whilst the followers of the Ionian team designated themselves the 'Spaldings' after a brand of golf clubs (which also form part of their arsenal). What began as healthy competition deteriorated into an intense rivalry. A girlfriend of one of the Spaldings was tampered with by one of the Fast Guns: bitter fighting broke out, a death followed and then killings began.

The Teenage Gangs
At predominately teenage level the male gangs form, numbering up to 50 members. Their age-range varies from 10-25 years old and they concentrate in various 'territories' in the Township, membership being determined largely by locality. Although there has been a proliferation of gangs into the Pangamen, Mau Maus, Vikings,

Molly McGuires, Young Americans, Mainstay and Butterflies (the last euphemistically named after their deadly butterfly-shaped choppers), the three which reign supreme are the Spaldings (often pronounced 'Sparlings'), Fast Guns, and Vultures (noted for their facial tattoos). The symbolic names of the gangs are graphic pointers towards an urge for power, dominance, virility and personal freedom; the original Mau Maus for instance were notorious for the killings they perpetrated in Kenya in the 1950's; Mainstay by contrast is a strong Cane Spirit.

Although the police pounce on the gangs periodically, girlfriends will silently hide the weapons and little boys are posted as early-warning systems, so fights tend to fizzle out miraculously at a moment's notice before the police arrive. Small boys in the Township have a detailed knowledge of gang activities and their hierarchical structure, and speak with awe of how the older boys roam the streets with pangas. Nine to 12 year old boys also form mini-gangs such as The Young Guns and The Young Riders: these serve as training grounds for real teenage gang activity.

It is a terrifying experience to be in the vicinity of a gang rampage, for their movements are silent but swift and sinister as a cheetah. In a moment knives, choppers and lethal home-made weapons flash out and the men break and form into little groups in pursuit of their victims.[9]

Fear of the Gangs

There are people in Western Township who are not bothered by the gangsters. Their attitude is 'if you keep to yourself they leave you alone'. At the same time, adults (men in particular) are constantly assaulted and robbed, especially at night and weekends. There are stabbing casualties weekly. Women are more frequently the victims of rape. People bar their doors and dislike venturing out at night. Nearly every family has felt or known the scars of the gangs and wives pass comments like: 'Well, we must do what we can now, because you can't tell how long a man will live here.'[10] One man relates how he was visiting a friend when suddenly a gang pounced on him and stabbed him in the eye: he has now lost his sight in it. Another nurses an arm that was 'chopped', another was pierced in the head by a screwdriver; he says he is alive, but sickly. The situation is endlessly repeated. Not only does it endanger the psychological equilibrium of the people of the Township, but for the new generation of Coloured children it is jeopardising the possibility of their father remaining an active breadwinner.

I am always struck by the fact that although adults fear the gangsters and feel they shouldn't go about harming people, at the same time they rarely stigmatise them or speak of them with negative emotional overtones. It is as though they regard the gang as an inanimate body which is harming people but because of continuous neutral face-to-face contacts with members individually and even in their homes, they know that at heart these boys are not criminals but just ordinary people who behave badly when in a group.

It would therefore seem that rehabilitative work with gangsters should be conducted via individual as well as group methods, and that constructive activities for children of different ages should be organised and incorporated in various community programmes.

Much gang violence is perpetrated in obedience to the rules of the group rather than as an overtly immoral act, and in general gang activities seem to result from a search for identity and security in a society which otherwise neglects its young people. One gangster who lives in a small two-roomed house with 16 other siblings, parents and kinsmen indicated that without his dagga-smoking (a practice that is rife among the gangs) his despair would be uncontainable.

Problems of Parenthood

Teenage life in most communities of the western world causes inter-generational tensions. These are exacerbated in Western Township by parental fears that their children's contacts will lead them to become gangsters or layabouts.

Thus one father tried to help his son by buying a car to prevent him from joining a gang, and in the process incurred considerable debt. A gang however forced the son to join them and used the car for their own purposes.

In another family the father would not allow his teenage daughter to go out at night because she could be stabbed. The parents refused to let her go to either of the two cinemas. Whenever she went out they wanted to know where she was going and with whom. This made her refuse to go out at all. Next the father found she was using birth-control pills. He got drunk, beat up his daughter and she had to go to hospital. The same father then bought a hi-fi set for his teenage children so that their friends would come to their home instead. They wouldn't. The mother bought an Encyclopaedia since she lacked the education to answer their questions. She paid this off at R5 a month (a real sacrifice), 'but they don't use it. I bought my daughter a set of Bible Stories and paid 50 cents a week HP but she's not interested and has never opened them. They're now all packed together in a box over there. All she wants is the picture-story books. I hate those picture-story books. They take their minds away from home and school. And they swop them all the time. If she finds half of one lying in the road, she goes and picks it up and reads that half!'

One Friday the daughter wanted to go out and the father refused to let her because he felt the man in question was of dubious character. On that occasion he had a violent argument with his daughter and beat her up again with the result that she left home and now does not return when he is there. Since then her father has taken to drinking even more heavily. 'He is very sentimental about his daughter and his heart is broken.' The mother is torn between the two.

Many fathers get furious if their sons join gangs. Depending on circumstances, some will relinquish gang-life, but others, even if they are sent to friends in another township, return to the streets again, much to their parents' despair.

The Effect of Distorted Relationships

The socialisation of children in every society is primarily the product of the calibre of life of the adult generation. As Rutter in his comprehensive evaluation of research into the effects of maternal deprivation has found: 'The association between disturbed family relationships and anti-social behaviour in the children is environmentally determined to a considerable extent.' (1973, p. 117) He concludes that: 'The studies into the development of anti-social behaviour in children show the importance of family relationships. Discord, tension and lack of affection in the home all appear to increase the likelihood of the children showing disorders of conduct. The exact mechanisms involved remain unclear, but it seems that father-mother and parent-child relationships are both influential, and that this effect is not necessarily associated with defects in attachment behaviour. **Distorted relationships**[11] rather than weak bonds seem to be responsible.' (p. 125)

Successful and Unsuccessful Parents

Since the mother plays the key-role in child-rearing, particularly during the early years, I have concentrated on her attitudes to a greater extent than those of the father, though as has been mentioned above the father is influential not only as a parent but in the quality of the relationship he shares with his wife or girlfriend.

Western Township like every place has its stock of successful and less successful mothers. The successful show their children affection, interest and tenderness, and communicate with them. Such mothers think for their children, allow the house to become a little untidy so that the children can feel at ease and play at home, work seven days a week if they have no money or food, and still try to care. They keep the children indoors on the cold winter mornings and listen to their noise with patience. The unsuccessful mothers lack the personal stability and equanimity of the former, are more self-centred and often are those weaker plants who become smothered by the weeds of slum-life: desertion, poverty, social disintegration, overcrowding and alcoholism. Some of these mothers are uncaring but others have the will to be good mothers but become too weighed down by circumstances. They exhibit a helplessness that accords with Hepner and Maiden's judgement on the inadequate mother: 'A mother may have the best intentions and desire to perform adequately, but her priority for this effort may be deflected by inundating life circumstances beyond her control.' (1971, p. 221)

One group of struggling mothers lives in a three-roomed house. Two teenage sisters board here, both are mothers of infants and receive no maintenance from their boyfriends. Tina (in her twenties) rents the house. She works in a globe factory, is unmarried and has a two year old son. She also allows her aunt and uncle, Mr and Mrs Coetzee, and their family to board there since they can't find accommodation elsewhere; they have five children.

Mr Coetzee is an alcoholic who works and gives his wife R2-R4 a week for all the food in the household. He earns R24 a month. Two of their children are malnourished and the youngest at 12 months has already been in hospital three times for gross malnutrition.[12] He and his wife have constant fights which become particularly vociferous over the absence of food and the demands of their young children. Mr Coetzee drinks nightly and on returning home normally argues with his wife and swears at the children saying he 'didn't ask to have a house full of children'. (He repeatedly throws away his wife's contraceptive tablets.)

Mrs Coetzee wants to put her eight year old son Gary into a 'home for safety' because he keeps running away from home. At night when the youngest baby cries, Mr Coetzee beats Gary until he wakes up. Then he tells him to shut the baby up. At other times the mother orders Gary to make up a bottle for this baby when she cries at night. During the day one finds this frightened eight year old cuddling and trying to care for the babies. The father kicks Gary because he is fond of his mother. He no longer goes to school.

Mrs Coetzee says she loves her children and is often affectionate towards them, at the same time she frequently leaves pots of boiling water on the floor even though one of her children has already been scalded in this way. Sometimes she will go out and find work and return only to buy her children R1 worth of sweets and chips, though they have no shoes and the weather is cold. She was not interested in a local sale of children's shoes where two pairs were selling for the price of one. Today Mrs Coetzee has lost interest in buying her children clothes. Instead, although she has few material objects or utensils except for four kettles, she obsessively continues to buy kettles and watch-straps for herself.

Mr and Mrs Coetzee have now reached the stage when Mrs Coetzee runs away from home and deserts all her children at the slightest provocation. She goes to a boyfriend in Pretoria by whom her youngest child was born.

The Coetzee children under these circumstances will clearly suffer from inadequate mothering as De Elejalde explains, for here are present: 'a rather ineffectual husband, many times a passive-aggressive man with symptomatic alcoholism' (p. 188) whose relationship with his wife is characterised by 'marital discord, mutual accusations and continued family feuds'. (1971, p. 188)

Tina (the niece who rents the house) has become so distraught with the constantly arguing parents and lack of food they give the children, that she has fought with them, left her 'own' house together with her baby, and is now living with the man who was first her mother's and then her elder sister's lover.

The Overcrowded Home

The plight of a little girl of seven who looks after her two younger sisters whilst her mother works should not pass unnoticed. In this one-roomed house live:

	Persons
Mother with boyfriend and their three children	5
Boyfriend's sister with boyfriend	2
Two old women addicted to methylated spirits	2
One old man	1
	10

At weekends there are invariably terrible fights in the household. The one child has not been vaccinated (and thus cannot attend school). She also has an uncoordinated eye. All the children fend for themselves. The overcrowding in such multi-problem households is acute[13] and because the women aren't married they are unlikely to be given a larger house to rent.

An Accumulation of Burdens

When one encounters families such as these one fears for the child. Neither the Departments of Social Welfare, Housing nor Recreation are coping with the problem, and the overcrowding, violence, ignorance and alcoholism continue. At the end of their study on disadvantaged children in Britain, Wedge and Prosser (1973, p. 59) make the obvious yet necessary point that 'what is striking is the massive accumulation of burdens afflicting disadvantaged children and their families, and which they are frequently expected somehow to overcome. Yet it should cause no surprise that so many of these children fail to "behave", fail to "learn", and fail to "succeed".'

Rutter maintains that: 'There is abundant evidence that mild mental retardation is extremely common among children brought up in city slums . . . [They are] more likely to live in disorganised overcrowded homes providing inadequate stimulation and educational opportunities . . . Intelligence develops, and is not a "given" capacity. Its development is a social process strictly dependent upon the quality and organisation of the human environment in which it evolves.' (p. 97)

An Ecological Problem

The problem is thus an ecological one, branching out into all areas of life that bear upon the child. For this reason I would urge wide-reaching social solutions tackling the root causes rather than the more obvious effects. First it is a matter of urgency that a committee for the uplift of Western Township be founded. Such a committee must involve the talents of the inhabitants and incorporate their desires in its functioning and aims. Perhaps the Coloured Representative Council could be operative in this. A branch of Marriage Guidance is required to improve marital and personal relations. I would urge that Child Welfare open an area branch to provide the much-needed crèches, and dental, medical and cultural care. Modern, practical Adult Education courses which can ripple out into 'neighbour teaching neighbour' programmes are necessary, advising parents on the handling of their children and bringing them into frequent contact with teachers in a constructive situation.

Children need to know that their homes and schools care for them, and the gangs need to know that social workers care more about them than do policemen. Once such priorities are established and the child and the individual become the centre of interest, and once their mothers and fathers are drawn together into community orientation and planning, only then can one foresee a future of hope for the Coloured child in Western.

FOOTNOTES

1. Accurate figures on illegitimacy in Western Township are not available, but the national figures for 1972, issued by the Minister of Statistics in 1974, reveal that it is a problem facing the Coloured community at large:
   White: 2 645
   Coloured: 32 296
   Asian: 1 928
   (Hansard, 3 col. 126, 19.2.1974; & 6 col. 401, 9.9.1974). This figure, of course, only records *officially registered* illegitimate births.
2.

Type of store	*Adult Buyer*	*Teenage Buyer*	*Child Buyer*	*Av. Amt. Spent*	*Time*
3 Butchers	101	44	96	R0,58	8 hours
1 Fruit and Vegetable	73	8	27	R0,21	2 hours
7 Grocers and General Dealers	269	66	770	R0,16	26 hours
Total:	443	118	893	R0,23	36 hours

3. All names used in the study are fictitious but representative of those found in the Coloured community.
4. See also p. 82, chap. 9 of this volume in relation to social work.
5. At present education is only compulsory if the parents have registered the child at the beginning of the year. No one is actively following up those who drop by the wayside as a result of failing to register.
6. *Robbery*=theft with threat of violence, as opposed to *larceny* (petty theft) and *burglary* (housebreaking with intent to steal).
7. South Africanism for cinema.
8. Corroborated by a newspaper report: *Rand Daily Mail,* 17. 5. 1975, p. 11.
9. In the middle of 1974 the leader of the Spaldings was hacked to death in hospital by the Vultures. In the early months of 1975 gang animosity soared dangerously high, until the press and a number of people tried to defuse their anger: subsequently an uneasy truce has persisted.
10. The life expectancy rate for Coloured men generally in South Africa is low. Figures given in a statistical news release from the Pretoria Bureau of Statistics on 9th December 1974 (p. 11) covering the period 1969-1971, were:

	Male	*Female*
White:	64,5	72,3 (yrs.)
Asian:	59,3	63,9
Coloured:	48,8	56,1

11. My emphasis.
12. 20–30% of the children of the Township are suffering from protein-calorie malnutrition. 20% of the under-two's are anaemic and 70% have an iron deficiency.
13. In August 1974 a report by the Department of Statistics, Pretoria, stated that during 1968-1971 the main causes of death among Coloured people were infective and parasitic diseases. These are closely related to poor and overcrowded living conditions.

Chapter 5
Marriage and Family Life

Workable Marriages

There are the happy, often religious marriages in Western such as those of Mrs de Wet who is 52 years old, has six children and was born an Anglican but changed to her husband's church, the Seventh Day Adventists, 'to keep peace'. Like many other Coloured women she accepts the church dictum that 'the man is the head but the woman is the neck' of the house. Many Coloured people summarise their household management and division of labour in similar phrases: 'The man is the head' and 'the woman is the pillar'. In practical terms this generally means that the man is responsible for finding paid employment and financing the household and the woman is responsible for caring for the children, food buying and preparation, clothing, health and housework.

In theory, most marital couples acknowledge the differentiation of duties and value of both sexes in performing their roles adequately as part of the modus operandi for a happy marriage and home. Although workable marital alliances are thus effected, very often such marriages tend not to evince much sharing or intimate communication. Many wives do not know what their husbands earn and husbands and wives do not discuss much: 'We are married, but he is a man and I am a woman and I do not ask him about his affairs', or 'the men drink one side, we on the other'. In such marriages one also finds a clear and distinctive philosophy concerning individual rights. The concept implies that every adult has a right to think and do what he wants within reason. Thus, though a woman vehemently disapproves of the fact that her husband is a heavy drinker, one frequently hears her say: 'Well I tried to change him and he didn't want to listen, so that's his affair.' The equanimity with which some marital couples are prepared to accept the 'do as I like' attitude of their partners is marked, though this is never encountered with regard to flirting, sex or extra-marital affairs.

There are good marriages and it is encouraging to come across them. They are like the 'Inn of Happiness'[1] where love pervades the selfless atmosphere and the wall-hanging symbolises the lives of the people: 'God does not take sides, He takes over.'

Problems in Marriage

Where husband and wife are able to accept and fulfil the male-female role differentiation one generally finds the basis for a successful marriage, but all too often external factors impinge and introduce a tension into the individual's perception and execution of his role.

The principal sources of conflict in marriages in the Township are:

(a) the home is overcrowded and inadequate, or the rentals too high;

(b) the Coloured woman is being caught up in the same emancipating process wrought by industrialisation as her counterpart all over the world and she desires to work for paid employment of her choice;

(c) the woman feels dissatisfied with her husband's performance in fulfilling his role as father and husband and therefore often enters his domain as breadwinner;

DEBS FRUIT & VEG. FRESH PRODUCE

(*d*) the man earns an inadequate wage because of his colour; he cannot always do the job he desires because of job reservation; he feels frustrated and humiliated at work and home, and becomes irritated and intolerant of his wife who does not understand his position and often demeans his manhood and self-esteem.

Many wives decide to go to work to supplement the family[2] income. This does not make it any easier for the man to accept his position. He feels increasingly redundant. Some men react to this situation with anger, some by being irresponsible, and others by trying to escape from it through drink.

It appears that the frustrations of the wife are closely related to the inability of her husband to provide for the family's physical needs, often linked to the changing role-expectation of women in general; whereas the problems of the husband largely derive from employment and socio-political disorientation.[3]

The Effect of Overcrowding

It is difficult for people who have not had to experience overcrowded housing without adequate facilities to appreciate the strain this brings into everyday relations. Housing conditions are a major source of tension in the Township. In her research on working and middle-class mothers in London, Gavron (1970, p. 58) states that: 'The quality of family life is greatly influenced by its standard of housing.' She goes on to quote the study of McGregor and Rowntree of 1962, who found that: 'Income and housing are the main indices of the quality of family environment especially when there are young children.'

Mr Haremse of the Township is frustrated beyond measure because of the overcrowding in his house. He and his wife live in three rooms with their three daughters and one son, all of whom have illegitimate infants in the house. Mr Haremse likes his privacy and needs to feel alone sometimes, 'but you cannot spend a minute without other people falling over you in this house. I have been on the waiting list for eight years to move to another, but the Rent Office just works by bribes and if ever we complain about the house, they tell us: "I'm not giving you a place for your furniture, I'm giving you a place for your family." So I say to them: You expect me to sit and eat on tomato boxes? Well I also like decent things to sit on. The walls of these houses get so wet, they don't even build airvents into them . . . I want to move to Eldorado Park on the Golden Highway, even if I have to pay R50 rent a month, but then they don't let you move where you want to.'[4]

The city environment in which the Coloured people find themselves, the pace of change and the demand for new workable attitudes also influence marriages adversely. Mr Haremse has an added problem. He is a devout Christian and a hardworker. But he walks through his home tense and aloof. Furthermore he and his wife are drifting apart because all their four teenagers are incessantly having illegitimate babies despite their orthodox religious upbringing. Mr Haremse feels smitten with guilt and rage because the grandchildren have all become **their** liability since none of the fathers will pay maintenance for them, and this has added to their overcrowding problem. His wife is 'soft' as he says, and has to wash, feed and care for them, though she suffers from a gnawing backache. Mrs Haremse runs away from home whenever her conflict between loyalty and regard for her husband and religion, and 'our children's mistake' becomes too great.

Mr and Mrs Isaacs, on the other hand, recall how they lived in the old neglected area of the Township for eight years. They had six children and the family lived in a three-roomed house. At that time Mrs Isaacs frequently became depressed and had to take sedatives: 'The cramped conditions got on my nerves.' Now they have moved to a spacious five-roomed row-house in the redeveloped area and 'this is paradise on earth. This is heavenly.' The Isaacs' maintain there has been an actual improvement in the happiness of family life with their change in living conditions.

Sexual intercourse

A large number of Western Township wives feel embarrassed about having sexual intercourse with their husbands because their children have to sleep in the same room. The whole situation requires caution, for as Aston and Dobson have found: 'Where the mother in the family was in some way inhibited or anxious about her sexual relationship with her husband,' she would tend to 'turn to her child for attention and satisfaction more often than did mothers who seemed to have made a better sexual adjustment to their husbands. This high degree of [mother]-child pairing probably served further to deflate the father's belief in his own value . . . thus a syndrome of disappointment appears to have been set up in these families, resulting in withdrawal on the part of the father and over-concern for the child on the part of the mother.' (1972, p. 88)

Certain parents find their way around this problem by putting all their children, except babies, in another room but 'I feel it's not right that my teenage sons and daughters sleep together and have to wash and dress together in the same room, but what can I do?' The importance of these areas of tension should not be underestimated and with such a constant exposure of children to sex and the opposite sex at vulnerable ages we should not feel surprise at rumours of incest around the Township, nor at the prevalence of promiscuity and illegitimacy.

The most common complaint about housing in the old area is the cramped conditions.[5] In most houses no more than three beds can be fitted in so the children either share a bed with one or more siblings or have to sleep lined up on newspaper on the floor of the lounge-cum-dining-room-cum-kitchen.

Childhood development

In addition to the negative consequences of crowding on parents and thus on the stability of family life, Plant (1963, pp. 510-513, 518-520) shows the detrimental effect it has on the personality development of children.

'Crowding seems very definitely to affect the self-sufficiency of children – their ability to be alone . . . It seems that persistent and constant crowding from early life destroys the sense of individuality.' Plant goes on to say: 'Our work in suburban and rural districts has convinced us that periods of being alone, of playing alone, of having the privacy of one's own room, are important fostering agents in a feeling of individuality, of self-sufficiency.'

Crowding serves to destroy the illusions which children build about other people. 'Images we build of others are the material of our dreams and goals. They are of great dynamic power – leading us to the best we can attain.' What happens in these overcrowded areas, says Plant, is that children 'do not want to follow in their fathers' footsteps,' they know them too well and they begin to distrust people.

In this respect he feels that crowding makes children become preoccupied with the sex **act,** rather than providing them with an understanding of coitus as a symbolic expression of a relationship, for they view the act before it has real meaning to them.

People in overcrowded conditions are subject to mental strain. They have a feeling that they 'want to get away from everybody'. 'When these periods of freedom are lacking' Plant goes on, there is either a 'somewhat forbidding negativism, or . . . irritable outbursts of temper which belong to the phenomena of fatigue . . . One sees a constantly recurring picture of "touchy" reactions and irritability . . . When we realise that for many . . . there is never a time that they are alone, we begin to get some picture of [the effect] this tension must [have]. Even the nights conspire to the same end: three to five children sleeping in the same bed means that even during the periods of relaxation and for the deeper levels of the unconscious there must always be this awareness of the imminence of others and the compromises and surrenders which this entails.'

Finally Plant has found that among people in crowded areas and families, there is what he calls 'the phenomenon of being so much in the world that there is no chance to look at it.' The ability to look objectively at oneself is of fundamental importance to the developing personality, but children and adults in these circumstances can rarely achieve more than a narrow, despondent subjectivism.

Rent and Wages: a Source of Friction

For that fifth of the Township fortunate enough to have been moved to the new area there is distinct relief at the housing improvement, even though Coloured people will take time to accustom themselves to living in flats. Unfortunately the accommodation is still not satisfactory because the rentals and electricity accounts are excessively high: one-third of the real income. Similarly Maasdorp reporting on rehousing of Africans in Durban, states: 'Although the new accommodation represents a substantial improvement on the old from the point of view of modern standards, the higher rentals involved exacerbate the already parlous economic position of the families.' (1975, p. 18)

Mr Willemse is a crane-driver. He has four children and earns a 'good' wage of R45 a week. This is his wife's budget: **Earnings** (pw) R45; **Expenditure** (pw) R64; Mrs Willemse's basic spending registers as: Rent – R15; Electricity (compulsory amount for flat dwellers) – R2; Groceries – R20; Meat (no roasts) – R8; Fruit and Vegetables – R3; and Furniture (HP) – R16. The weekly deficit is thus R19. Either the family is bedevilled by debt, or, as usually happens, Mrs Willemse has to work to make good the deficit.

I frequently met families in this zone where frictions arose over a trivial remark such as Mrs Willemse asking her husband if they could buy another chair as people always had to find a box to sit on when visiting. He flared up in anger at this suggestion and shouted: 'O K, so go and find yourself another husband if I'm not good enough for you. I can't get better money, I can't give it; go and find someone who will give it to you.'

The men in the redeveloped zone are generally earning better wages than in the old area but they are still tense and easily irritated because as husbands and fathers they cannot provide adequately. This feeling of failure, exacerbated by the wife's often tactless remarks because she battles to make ends meet and also wants some modern conveniences, is at the root of much marital discord.

In 1956 it was said that 'poverty is the chief cause of the lack of homes, and the Coloured people have, on the whole, been unable to afford to buy or build houses for themselves.' (C.P.C. & A.J. Housing for Coloured People 1956, p. 21) Professor S. P. Cilliers has stressed the same factors in broader perspective: 'The major social problems amongst Coloureds are directly related to their socio-economic position and centre around poverty and housing. It therefore concerns the provision of basic necessities of life.' (1971, p. 35)

Implications of the Working Wife

In their discussion of American family structure, Queen and Habenstein (1967, pp. 303-304) observe that: 'Along with these changing roles have come challenges to the earlier male dominance.' Sometimes the male still makes the important decisions and has the power, in other cases the wife-mother is dominant whilst in still others there is partnership. 'All too often there is conflict and something of a power struggle.

Perhaps even more often there is confusion and ambivalence, with both husband and wife uncertain as to division or sharing of labour, authority, and responsibility. These uncertainties contribute to instability in many American families.'

Some Western Township wives and mothers desire to work in paid employment because of the liberation it affords them from endless household chores. They enjoy the stimulation of a change of environment and people, can fulfil themselves in a job they like, and can buy the little luxuries that give them pleasure. But even if the wife explains that her being employed is no reflection on her husband's ability, most husbands resist this consciously or subconsciously because they know that employment out of the home makes their wives less economically and emotionally dependent on them, and because it complicates household management, often leading to a sharing of chores and blurring of traditional sex-linked behaviour patterns.

Eva and her husband, Sam, are both 29. They have two children. Eva gets Sam's full wage of R47 a week, does all the budgeting and then gives him a bit as 'pocket money'.

Sam comes from an unstable home – of his brothers, one is a drunkard, one was imprisoned and one has run away. His mother died when he was young, his father is an alcoholic, and Eva feels 'you can't expect him to be different, but it does get me down'.

Soon after they were married Sam began to go about with other women. He was also caught and sentenced to two years and seven months for theft. When he was imprisoned Eva brought her two children to her mother's home in Grasmere and returned to try and complete her nursing studies. She is an auxiliary nurse. When she was about to write her finals Sam was released from prison. Although she tried to evade him, he found where she was living and threatened her saying she was still his wife, so they moved into his uncle's house in Western. She had to abandon her studies.

Eva was born a Roman Catholic but on marriage changed over at Sam's request to the Ou Apostoliek Kerk. (It is a Coloured practice in the area that the wife should if necessary leave her religion for the husband's.) Sam is a priest of this church, and one day a week they have prayers at people's houses, another day they take the sacraments, another pay home-visits. Virtually every night there is some activity concerning the church. It forbids alcohol and smoking. When Sam passes through his religious phase, life is easier and he stops drinking but then suddenly he develops a craving for liquor and has a drinking bout. Then he drinks and drinks 'for weeks on end'. His behaviour is inconsistent.

Matters are not improved by Sam's *'Omie'* (Uncle), the 'owner' of the house, being constantly drunk and out of work. The uncle left his job because he refused to work for 'Kaffir wages', then a car knocked him down in a hit-and-run accident, so he has given up and spends his life – as do many of the very lost and very poor – drinking Methylated Spirits and *White Malmsey* (White Wine).

Eva says she is unused to such living and hates it when this '*Omie* just hangs about and gets drunk'. The uncle's son also lives there, also gets drunk and is looking for work. Sam's father used to live there too: he used to spend most of the day flopped out on the couch.

Although it is the uncle's 'house', Sam and Eva pay the rent. Sometimes Sam becomes angry and tells Eva not to serve food for his uncle and son because they are contributing nothing to the household. But then she feels guilty at just cooking for the two of them and their children and prepares a little extra, leaving it in the pot so they can take it out if they want to.

Sam hasn't any table or other manners and although Eva tried to teach him she feels he won't learn because he was never taught these in his home. On one of my visits they had another argument because she opened her wardrobe and all his clothes came tumbling out. This made him angry: 'There you go swearing at me again.' 'But I must because you won't learn these manners.' 'He always just throws his stuff on the cupboard whereas he should neatly fold and hang them.'

Eva meets with the other women of the Apostolic Church once a week in the morning for Bible and prayer groups and finds this pleasant, but generally she keeps to herself. She was learning how to crochet a cap from her African domestic servant, as 'I must find something to do and I can't find a pattern'. At night she reads the picture-books her husband buys her and 'Living and Loving'.[6] Eva won't go to the cinema if Sam wants to take her out at night because she's too afraid of being attacked by Western gangsters.

Eva has told Sam that she feels they must get rid of their domestic servant[7] because they could benefit from the extra money to cover their hire-purchase expenses. They bought a bedroom suite for R800 [8] and have to pay off R40 a month. She says the firm is very strict and if you neglect payment for one month, they just take the things away. (The uncle had a kitchen unit, had paid half but got into arrears so the firm concerned removed it.)

Sam and Eva's biggest disagreement centres around the fact that 'he won't let me go and get work and I'm bored stiff at home. He wants me to be a Lady!' In their very small three-roomed house she therefore has a domestic servant who does everything, while Eva does nothing. 'So I tell him, if he wants me to be a Lady, then he must also give me the clothes that go with a lady – and a few Rand for my pocket every day so that I can go and spend them on what I like in town.' Eva wants to return to nursing, but Sam finds night-shift totally unacceptable.

Over-Possessive Men

Linked with the Coloured man's general sense of insecurity and the poor communication between people in the area, is the phenomenon of hyper-possessiveness which Marsden also observed in a study of mothers who now live alone in Britain. 'A much more serious problem [than unfaithfulness] for about a quarter of the wives was the husband's acute sexual jealousy, which was part of his attempt to control the wife's social life.' (1973, p. 87)

The following case-study demonstrates the torn fabric of these relationships and the feelings of bondage which accompany them. It is representative of a number of others in which man and woman become so distraught at their inability to reach one another that the man erupts in violence and the woman forgets everything, even her children, and runs away to a friend – thus desperately trying to find herself and regain her perspective on life. Although the account may at times become somewhat melodramatic it is necessary to take cognisance of what the woman is saying and how she says it for these reflect the intense emotional disturbance which she is experiencing.

Lucy, 26, is petite and pretty. Her home is in Douglasdale but she does not want to return there for she needs money to support her children. Lucy has lived with Tom for nine years and has had two living children by him: '*Maar in al die tyd het hy nog nooit gedink om 'n ring op my vinger te sit nie.*' ('But in all this time he has never thought of putting a ring on my finger.') '*Hy is vreeslik jaloers, en hy slaat en slaat my totdat die bloed by my uitkom . . . Jy kan vir jouself sien.*' ('He is terribly jealous, and he beats and beats me until he draws blood . . . You can see for yourself.') She showed me gashes on her arm, a host of scars disfiguring her face and head and a burn-like mark on her cheek. '*Nee dis nie brand nie, hy het my met sy tekkie gestamp.*' ('No, it's not a burn, he hit me with his tennis-shoe.')

Tom does not give her much money, '*dan gaan ek was en stryk en ek skrub die vloere om net 'n bietjie geld vir my kinders te kry. Ek sê vir jou suster ek weet nie meer wat om te doen nie, ek het 'n slegte lewe.'* ('Then I go and wash and iron and scrub floors just to get a little money for my children. I tell you sister, I no longer know what to do, I have a bad life.') *'Ek móet my mooi aantrek en skoon klere aansit om te werk, al gaan ek om was te doen. Dan word hy kwaad en sê ek sit daardie klere aan om met ander mans rond te loop. Hy is so jaloers.'* ('I must dress nicely and put on clean clothes to work, even though I go to do washing. Then he becomes angry and says I put on those clothes to flirt around with other men. He is so jealous.')

Lucy should have had three children but had one miscarriage. When she was expecting the first child she and Tom had an argument. He was sitting in the back-yard drinking with friends. She was six months pregnant. He first threw a tin at her stomach and then hit her until she forced herself under the sofa to hide. *'Ek lê in Baragwanath vir drie maande. Ek het baie bloed verloor want ek het baie worries. Maar dank die Here ek het nog twee ander kinders.'* ('I lay in Baragwanath [hospital] for three months. [Probably an exaggeration.] I lost much blood because I have a lot of worries. But thank the Lord I still have two other children.')

She has now run away from him to a friend's house for they have had another crisis but she says: *'Al lag ek en sê ek sal weg bly, my hart is baie seer en ek wonder hoe my kinders is; ek kan nie eet nie, vandag eet ek al niks nie, want ek wonder wat sal hulle eet. Dit maak my baie hartseer om te dink dat my kinders daar alleenig is. En die mense sal ook sê, watter soort moeder is ek wat my kinders so verlaat? Ek weet nie wat om te doen nie.'* ('Although I laugh and say I shall stay away, my heart is very sore and I wonder how my children are; I can't eat, today I have eaten nothing, because I wonder what they will eat. It makes me very heartsore to think that my children are alone there. And the people will also say, what kind of mother am I that deserts her children? I don't know what to do.')

Lucy does not complain of Tom wanting sexual intercourse every night as some other women do: *'Hy is nie so 'n lover nie. Dis net die slater. Hy is 'n slater.'* ('He isn't such a lover. It's just the hitting. He is a [wife-] beater [a bully].) She feels Tom has acted irresponsibly towards her *'want hy het my 'n vrou gemaak'* ('because he made me a woman'). *'Ek sê altyd, hierdie slum trouery is niks nie. Ek dink nou dis baie beter om by 'n court te gaan om met die pampiere te trou. Jy het niks met die slum trou nie.'* ('I always say this slum marriage is nothing. I now think it's much better to go to a court to marry with the papers. You have nothing with this slum marriage.')

Now Lucy says: *'Ek wil met 'n óu man trou wat net by my sal bly en geselskap gee, en my help na my kinders kyk. Ek wil nie meer hierdie jong mans hê nie. Ek dink dit sal beter wees.'* ('I want to marry an **old** man who will just stay with me and give me company, and help me care for my children. I no longer want these young men. I think that would be better.')

Lucy has reported Tom to the Welfare Department a long time ago – *'maar dis so lastig en jy moet weer en weer gaan voor hulle [die Welsyn] iets doen. En as jy nie getroud is nie sal hulle jou net 'n kamer gee vir jouself en jou kinders . . . Dis nie O K nie, jy kan nie die res van jou lewe net jou kinders geselskap hou. Watter soort geselskap is hulle!'* ('But it's so tiresome and you have to go again and again before they [the Welfare] do anything. And if you aren't married they will only give you a room for yourself and your children. It's not O K, you can't just have companionship with your children for the rest of your life. What kind of companionship are they!')

Marsden's mothers in Northborough and Seaston (UK) had the same problems: They 'felt they lacked somebody to talk to about adult matters, sex, the neighbours' (p. 143); and they reported somewhat prejudicial aid from the authorities who tended to discriminate against unmarried mothers. (1973, pp. 247, 258–259 and 283)

Distrust between Sexes

There is a good deal of distrust between husbands and wives, and acts of infidelity are not infrequent. In conversation it is noticeable how people often classify their spouses with a stereotyped image of the opposite sex and show a better understanding of and closer affinity towards members of their own sex. The Lynds found a similar pattern in their study of life in a typical small American city. In many working class families 'the necessities of shelter and food overshadow other plans; such conversation as there is may be of a bickering sort, or may lapse into apathetic silence . . . This frequent lack of community of interests, together with the ideas each sex entertains regarding the other, appears in many families in a lack of frankness between husband and wife, far-reaching in its emotional outcome.' (1929, p. 120)

Such behaviour not only prevents intimate communication and mutual sharing between the sexes on matters other than sex and organisational trivia, but it affects the children. As Lidz (1973) so rightly emphasises, the family is the dynamo of personality development and its aberrations; it is here that essential values pertaining to marriage, parenthood, male and female are formed. The problem of male violence and female back-chat is as real in Western as it is in the working-class north of England; though here the in-built safeguards of humour are perhaps not as extensively developed. However, the mutual inability to discuss things honestly and gently with a desire to understand the other's position is common to both.

Dorothy is 38 and has been married for 12 years. Both she and her husband, Herman, are from Johannesburg. She works as a table-hand *'want ek het moeilikheid by die huis'* ('because I have problems at home').

A few years ago Dorothy thought Herman was having an affair with another woman. His sister, who lives next door, spoke to him and he left the woman. Their marriage improved for a short time. Now he isn't 'going on with another woman but he is terrible to me'. Dorothy does not think it is only Herman who is like this but that **all** men in Western Township have become like this. *'Ek weet nie wat met hierdie mans aangaan nie, hulle was nie altyd so – ek dink daar is net een of twee mans in Western wat goed is, dis al.'* ('I don't know what's the matter with these men; they were not always like this – I think there are only one or two men in Western who are good, that's all.')

Dorothy's marital problems have been aggravated since September 1974 when Herman was attacked by gangsters when he was coming home from a drink: they wanted to take his money; he refused. In fending them off they stabbed and injured his left arm so seriously that he had to leave off work. They also broke the bone and it became septic. The doctor said he would have to find lighter work. Herman was out of work until February 1975 when he found a job but was fired because his arm was not strong enough for him to work satisfactorily. He now has a light job nearby but is only earning R20 a week. Every time his arm becomes painful he bullies the family and Dorothy feels because he got stabbed he now hits and beats her and wants to hurt the children as well. He is especially violent when drunk. She has a head-scar where he struck her with a chopper. Every morning and evening she rubs and binds the arm for him.

Of the money Herman earns Dorothy only gets what he gives her (R1 or R2 a week) despite the cost of living and their six children. Therefore she works. She doesn't know what he does with the rest of the money but he spends a lot on drink.

Although she struggles financially, her overriding concern is her marriage. She feels helpless about it. Some days he beats her up so badly that her face is too swollen for her to go to work. She is fortunate in having an understanding supervisor who overlooks these absences, *'sy verstaan, want sy het ook 'n swaar lewe gehad.'* ('She understands, because she has also had a hard life.')

One day, after another conjugal fight, the eldest daughter of 12 remonstrated with her father upon which he half-strangled her. Dorothy went straight to the Newlands police and brought him before 'the Peace'. Herman received a warning which had only a temporary effect. Dorothy then asked Herman's father to speak to him – this too was of no avail. Before one of my visits he had taken a plate of food she had prepared for him and thrown it to the dogs. This is a vehement and fairly common symbolic display of anger used by husbands against wives in the Township, for food is not only scarce but the act of eating together can reinforce familial ties.

Drink and Marriage

Alcohol is a further aggravator of marital tension. The implications of alcoholism on family life as stressed by SANCA[9] are: *(a)* the important roles of each family member may be distorted ie the mother may have to compensate for the father's lack of leadership and this affects her relationship to her husband and children and the children have to adapt to a poor father-figure; *(b)* normal family behaviour becomes distorted; *(c)* values and standards held by the family seem to disintegrate; *(d)* the spouse becomes so absorbed in her partner's drinking that little energy and thought remain for the children's development; *(e)* personal difficulties with the partner are exacerbated.[10] (nd pp. 4-5)

Although there are sociologists who maintain that alcohol is not a cause of marital disintegration, and although many Coloured men and some women regard drinking as a legitimate and basic form of cultural recreation, it is evident that the pattern of alcoholic drinking in the Township is a major source of family unhappiness.

Mrs Mostert is 46. She separated from her first husband as he gave her no money and they couldn't agree on anything. Her second husband earns 'good money' – R50 a week.[11] He gives her half his wages for running the household: she does not know what he does with the rest. Her husband believes housework 'is just for women. If a pot is cooking, he calls me to tell me it is boiling over; he will never think of taking it off the stove. He doesn't lift a finger in the house.' He drinks heavily at weekends and then fights with people, especially her adult son by her first marriage who is also an alcoholic.

From Monday to Thursday Mr and Mrs Mostert eat together in the kitchen-cum-dining-room. But on Fridays and weekends they virtually do not see one another as he is 'up and down, up and down'[12] in the Township. She now leaves his supper cooked on the stove and he comes and eats it when he pleases.

Mr Mostert's drinking wears his wife down: 'you don't find good husbands here.' Their irritations are increased because he wishes to have sexual intercourse nightly, whilst she only wants it once a week: 'I get so cross because men are just too sexy. They just want sex all the time. My husband works hard and he even works overtime but he still wants sex. When he's like that I get fed-up and I go to make some tea. This makes him mad and he chases me about the house and throws things and says I don't want sex because I'm having it with other men . . . This isn't true, I'm just not so sexy.'

When her husband's and son's alcoholism depress her, Mrs Mostert often thinks: 'Why is my life so? What did I do wrong? I think about it often . . . Maybe, it's like the Bible says – that we are being punished for the sins of our forefathers. I don't know. I get no answer . . . but there is no true love between people.'

Disillusionment with Marriage

There is an increasing number of people in the Township who have seen or experienced broken marriages or conjugal violence, and this has set them against marriage as a form of partnership. Not only does this have the effect of proliferating the number of fatherless children, but the mothers do not have the resources to provide for them adequately.

Patsy is about 50. Her husband is dead but gave her such a hard life beating her and refusing to talk to her that she never wants to marry again. She is contented just to live in her little house of two and a half rooms with her grandchildren and women friends who visit. Once they've had *"n bietjie geselskap'* ('a bit of companionship') they leave again, and *'ek gee die kinders 'n bietjie kossetjie en sit hulle in die bed, dan is ek tevrede.'* ('I give the children a little food and put them to bed. Then I am satisfied.')

She has four daughters and a son. The son is in prison for 'bad company'. The daughters are not married though all have children, and the men don't want to pay maintenance. Patsy receives R80 a month from the Welfare Department to look after the four children, though she finds it too little to manage on. Her daughters don't want to marry because they say men aren't interested in marriage nor would they treat them well.

Implications for the Children

What is evident from the foregoing data is that many marriages in the Township are emotionally unstable or brittle. Not only has this kind of environment serious implications for the partners concerned but also for the socialisation and exposure of the children. The McCords (1960, p. 108) have emphasised that: 'The general emotional tone of a family is largely governed by the nature of the relationship between parents.'

The state of human relationships as expressed in the conjugal tie in Western is a cause for concern. If, as it seems, marriage in urban settings throughout the world is becoming increasingly meaningless in the **institutional** sense (Queen and Habenstein, 1967, p. 311) then its role as a vehicle for human affection and companionship assumes greater importance. We need therefore to work at the conditions and attitudes which block effective communication and mutual pleasure between partners. Marital disruption is so real and so unresolved in the Township that the young people are rapidly losing faith in marriage as an institution specifically, and in human relations generally. Furthermore its value as a positive nurturing ground for the young is being seriously threatened, and they are receiving inadequate alternative security and affection.

Marriage in the Social Context

Consequently factors militating against effective family life must be countered. A crash programme of improved housing is necessary with the Department of Community Development taking note of the demographic and social consequences of such schemes as have been undertaken in similar circumstances in other countries. Sociological source books recommended by specialists in the field are invaluable guides.

Marriage guidance clinics could be established with the help of both qualified psychiatrists on an advisory basis, and local volunteers (eg teachers, businessmen, and even shebeen owners) not only to help people in dire need of counselling but to encourage healthy adult interaction between the sexes.

Adult education lectures, discussions, group meetings and films need to be initiated to lift the morale and interest level of the community, tackling themes perplexing the people and affecting the socialisation of their children.

In this respect I feel it is necessary for social workers to direct their energies towards community problems that affect the personal lives of hundreds of individuals in an area, rather than solely administering to the few who come to their notice.[13]

FOOTNOTES

1. The name a young married couple have given to their home. House-names are rare in the Township.
2. The sample studied indicates that household composition primarily consists of the nuclear family.
3. The man's sources of frustration are more fully dealt with in chapters 6 and 7.
4. Mr Haremse works independently as a mechanic. Houses are held back in such cases by the Department as the income is deemed 'unsteady'.
5. Two-roomed houses are normally 27,9 m^2; the largest are four-roomed units totalling 37,3 m^2.
6. A white-oriented magazine popular in the Township. It contains useful advice on all matters related to child-rearing.
7. 30% of the mothers in the random sample were found to have African domestic servants whom they pay an average of R6–R7 a week. However a new law forcing them to have servants with a valid pass for the Johannesburg area, to register them and give them annual paid leave, is reducing the numbers. Although most of the inhabitants regard this law as being yet another aspect of political discrimination, it has the positive side of also providing a limited form of protection against exploitation by the employer.
   Most of the Coloured inhabitants in Western Township are poor and they are employing domestic servants at a wage not even half that of the current MEL (see p. 58). When questioned, the people rationalise the situation by saying that the amount is more than most whites are paying their servants and if they do not employ these Africans they would not have jobs so they are doing them a service. Clearly a compulsory liveable minimum wage for domestic servants and employment regulations need to be introduced to protect these workers. If people cannot afford to pay full-time servants properly, they should be paid by the hour or have other employment. It is understandable that many of the inhabitants wish to spend up to R800 on a lounge or bedroom suite, but it is not condonable that they fail to pay their servants adequately.
8. There is a general tendency towards spending above one's means in the Township. Almost all household furniture purchases are on the credit system and 63% of families in the old area are weighed down with debts and repayments. Many people are trying to emulate the life-style of the whites. Whereas in the poor homes there is usually a bed, a rickety table and broken chair or box; in the redeveloped area (the row-houses and flats) a chronic status race is underway. This behaviour may in fact be an attempt to attain a personal sense of worth via material possessions; for a feeling of belonging and status are not easily attainable for Coloured people in other ways.
9. The South African National Council on Alcoholism and Drug Dependence, a welfare organisation run on the basis of Alcoholics Anonymous.
10. SANCA nd *When Alcoholism Strikes — A Practical Guide for the Family.*
11. The average wage in the Township old area is R78,24 a month, but much of the money goes on alcohol.
12. A commonly repeated phrase suggestive of restlessness in the Township.
13. See chapter 9 which discusses this problem in some detail.

Chapter 6
Work, Wages and Productivity

As explained in chapter 1 the people of the Township are predominantly engaged in semi-skilled and skilled activities though a small proportion is involved in administrative and clerical work. The median **monthly** income in 1974 for full-time work by individuals was R78,24 for the old area and R146,20 for the redeveloped zone.[1]

Importance of a Good Wage

The foremost reason given for leaving jobs was low pay. Edelstein in his attitudinal study of Coloured people in Johannesburg also found that the main grievance of 73% of his middle-class[2] sample was unequal pay for equal work, whilst the second (67% of his sample) was inadequate opportunities for employment ie the application of job reservation on racial lines. (1973, pp. 250–251)

Mr Brandt is an assistant to an electrician and earns R12 a week. His wife has always had to work *'want ons is armoedige mense'* ('because we are deprived people'). They have four children. Sometimes Mrs Brandt wishes she could just be a housewife. Until recently she was a garment worker earning R13 a week but has left that job because it strained her eyesight. Now she works in a lighting company 'packaging with the clever machines' and earns R16 a week.

Miss Boukamp, a young mother of 16, left work to give birth to her baby. She won't return to her former employer, a Johannesburg stocking manufacturer *'want die geld is te min'* ('because the money is too little') – she was earning R14 a week. She wants to work again because her divorced mother is an alcoholic and beats her. She becomes restless at home and needs money. However her grandmother, who also lives in the house, says that the (illegitimate) baby is too young to be left on its own and as she is getting old now and wants a bit of time to herself she is reluctant to care for it.

Mr Larsons is 20 years old and has an illegitimate child whom his parents are caring for. He works for a battery company on the Witwatersrand earning R25 a week. He feels the money he is paid is too little for the type of work he does, especially as the firm does not provide workers with protective clothing or gloves, and the hair on his legs and arms is already burnt away by acid. Every time the workers ask for gloves they are promised them but 'they never arrive'.

Mr Philips, a young man of 18, has had two jobs, one at a tea factory, the other at a pie factory. In each case he earned R15 a week and left because the pay was too low and his employers refused to raise his wage. He and his mother are racking their brains as to how to get him out of the Township because one of the strong teenage gangs is operative in his area and will attack him if he stays around during the day and does not join them.

Mrs Carlisle has seven children and nine years of happy marriage, but felt she had to go to work as her husband was earning R25 a week and they could not meet the cost of living on this amount. Her husband shows resentment at his wife needing to work, knowing that she is satisfied as a housewife caring for the children. This has become a source of marital friction.

For these people at the bottom of the wage ladder the mere struggle to obtain sufficient money for food and shelter is an energy-consuming activity. For those at the top, over a third of the wage is swallowed up by the high cost of living in the redeveloped area. In both areas there is evidence of overspending on household equipment and alcohol, and I frequently met families in which the husband was earning R20 a week but only gave his wife R2-R4 for food for the family.

Unemployment

Another feature of the Township is its high number of unemployed. Fifty per cent of the sample adults of the old area had been unemployed for a period of two weeks or more in the two years prior to the study.

Mr Moss is 36 and a boiler-maker. He has been out of work for four months since he was laid off as redundant. He wants another job and has walked the streets trying to find one, but without success. He belongs to a Trade Union: 'They tell you of jobs like one in Isando, and you go there and find there is no longer a job.'

At present he is impecuniously sitting around in the house of his parents, who through their staunch religious convictions try to raise his morale and forbid him to turn to alcohol. He has a house and is married with five children, but since he has been out of work his wife has refused to let him return home. She has now gone to work. 'It makes me feel bad because my children come to visit me at weekends and I haven't even got a cent to give them.'

High Job Turnover

Coloured people 'have in the past been excluded from many occupations in the Transvaal through racial prejudice on the part of both White employers and White workers, and through "job reservation" . . . and other governmental measures. Many White employers tended to have stereotypes of Coloured workers as unreliable, irresponsible, lazy and physically weak, and preferred Africans for manual work and Whites for skilled work'. (Randall and Burrow, 1968, p. 31)

Despite such earmarking I constantly came across Coloured men and women saying in rather sanguine fashion: 'Oh I **enjoy** working and I work hard. I left because of my backache. But even now they're still waiting for me there.'

Mrs Mackenzie worked on parachutes for two years at R17 a week. She found her job light and enjoyed it but left because her child was thin and weak. A year later she found work at a canvas company at R21 a week which she preferred. She likes working but claims that '*as ek werk is my hart by my kinders*' ('when I work my heart is with my children.')

Other mothers report similar experiences and will stay away from work if they or their children are feeling ill. They are unaware that their absence from work for a day or week might affect the employment situation. Some of the mothers studied in depth had the high turnover of three jobs a year. Van der Merwe recently estimated (1974, p. 37) that the loss to a company employing unskilled workers is R133 per separation. Not only is this costly for the economy, but generally during unemployment such earners and their families have no financial assistance.

The Case of Mrs Venter

Mrs Venter is 46 years old and illiterate. She has had four jobs since the beginning of 1974. She was first a seamstress for a well-known Johannesburg firm of dressmakers, and worked for them for a number of months for R10 a week. She left her job because 'the money was too little', then she found employment at a factory and worked for one month earning R14 a week. She left that job because she developed severe abdominal pains and was admitted to hospital for treatment. Her last job was working for a chemical firm where her wage was R10 a week, but she was usually paid R17 as she worked overtime all day Saturday and Sunday – a seven day week.

Mrs Venter has seven children and the family lives in two tiny rooms for which she pays R6 a month rent. The family's daily menu is:

Breakfast: Thin porridge and sugar, black tea and sugar.
Lunch: 'The children have lunch if friends give to them.'
Supper: Porridge, tomatoes, onions, and fish-oil.
(Minced meat or 'soup bones' [ribs] are eaten once a week.)

She is the sole supporter of the family. Her husband has been out of work for two years and nine months since the time he was hit on the head by gangsters in the Township and in consequence had a brain haemorrhage. He has been ill and confused since that time. He is usually found lying on a torn mattress with a blanket over him. He has lost the will to live.

The Social Welfare Department will not assist the family with maintenance because they say Mr Venter is fit to work. He used to be a painter earning R14 a week although he would only give his wife R5 out of that for groceries and did not consider it her affair to know what he did with the rest. Before his unemployment he was an alcoholic but since they have had no money he tends to be without friends or drink.

Mrs Venter's eldest son of 19 is serving a two and a half year prison sentence in Pretoria's Central Prison 'for bad company' – he was the driver of a stolen vehicle. She speaks of him regretfully for 'he was the only person who used to help me feed and clothe the family'. Her second eldest son is *'ongeskik'* (rude/disrespectful). He swears at both his parents, and left school because he was involved in a car accident nine years ago. Now they don't know what he does with his life. The third eldest son of 16 would like to go to school. The Headmaster says Mr Venter does not want him to go; Mr Venter says the Headmaster refuses to admit him. These two sons were sleeping in a deserted car in the Township in winter having 'left home' temporarily. The fourth eldest son of 14 is still at home but on the street: he says the school does not want him; *'Freddie en sy pa sit nie langs een vuur nie'* ('Freddy and his father do not sit alongside the same fire' [ie don't get on].) He sells newspapers in the City centre on Saturday nights to try to earn a little money. The two daughters of eight and nine attend the double-session primary school at different times, and the youngest son of five is still at home though he says he would like to go to a crèche. Normally Mr and Mrs Venter sleep in one single bed, the two girls and little brother in another, and when they are at home the three teenage sons in another.

Mrs Venter says she hasn't had a happy day since she married 18 years ago. She likes employment, but when she works, her children and the washing preoccupy her mind. Claudia, the nine year old daughter, does the family washing because Mrs Venter doesn't have time to wash clothes and can't afford a servant. They have only three blankets in the house and use dirty clothes for warmth on cold winter nights.

I not infrequently met her children in various parts of the Township rummaging rubbish bins for empty beer bottles in order to use the deposits to buy food. Mrs Venter has also started drinking 'because of my worries'. Though she realises it doesn't solve her problems, it temporarily helps her to forget. One week in winter her struggles so overwhelmed her that I heard her saying: *'Ek wil my onder 'n trein of kar gooi, ek kan dit nie meer verdra nie.'* ('I want to throw myself under a train or car, I can't bear it any longer.')

It was a freezing day, there was no coal or food in the house, the only item being a small packet of washing powder. Mrs Venter had bad flu and her son Freddy who had had 'ammonia' (pneumonia) was coughing terribly. She couldn't go to the Hospital Outpatients because she hadn't 50 cents and she felt too sick to go to work. I gave her 50 cents for the hospital and 50 cents for food, upon which she immediately sent her five year old son to buy 10 cents paraffin, 10 cents mielie-meal, 10 cents sugar, 10 cents 'soup bones' with 10 cents over. The next day whilst interviewing, the five year old Hennie came and jubilantly called out: *'Juffrou, ons het geëet!' 'O wonderlik! En wat het julle geëet?' 'Juffrou, gisteraand het ons pap geëet, en, en ons het melk gehad, Juffrou.'* ('Miss, we ate!' 'O wonderful! And what did you eat?' 'Miss last night we ate porridge, and, and we had milk, Miss.') That same day Mrs Venter was fired from her job for too much absenteeism.

Since that time the Labour Department has found Mr Venter a job doing sheltered light carpentry work at one of the mining houses, for which he is paid R35 a month. But his attendance is haphazard. Mrs Venter has had to stop working: she has developed severe stomach-ache, is receiving hospital treatment for an ulcer, and is weak and ill. She now weighs 30 kg.[3]

Understanding between Employer and Employee

Although the wage a worker gets is of paramount importance as it affects what his family eats and wears, the medical care they can afford, whether they can go away on holiday and, within government policy, what type of house and area they can live in, there are important side-effects of the worker's home environment that are often overlooked.

An individual's identity is composed of the sum total of roles he or she plays, of which the employee role is but one (though highly important), and identities fall into different patterns depending on the ecological systems in which people operate. Thus people from Western Township are likely to come to work with certain environmental experiences in common.

An example is Mrs Richardson who makes cement bags and earns R15 a week out of which she must pay R6 for a nanny to care for her 18 month old baby. She has two other children. Her husband earns R30 a week, pays the R6 rent and, incredibly spends all except R3 on drink. This R3 of his weekly wage he gives her for household groceries. They have many violent quarrels and Mrs Richardson was out of work for two weeks because of black eyes and wounds but she says: 'My boss knows my domestic troubles, he understands,' and he tolerates her absences. Here one finds the beginnings of an employer-employee relationship.

Coloured employees spontaneously expressed real gratitude to good employers who take into account the **home environment** in their business relationship.

Employment Formalities

Because the adults of Western Township have little experience of paperwork they often find themselves trapped by employment formalities which they do not fully understand.

Mrs de Kok is a cashier at a supermarket and earns R19 a week. She is on unpaid sick-leave because she had not worked for the store for 13 weeks when she became ill. 'The form was so complicated, I didn't know it meant I wouldn't get benefits.' She, her two children, her elder brother and his two children are at present all living off their parents' R47 a month[4] combined pension. Mrs de Kok had been hit on the head by gangsters, as had her husband who subsequently left her, smashed up their furniture, and then hanged himself. She feels she 'must go and work for money for my children but I feel sick in the head'. Mrs de Kok still has a debt of R13 to pay to a medical concern in the city and is very distressed at the threatening letters she keeps receiving from them, as her father helplessly explains: 'These people, they don't understand if you tell them your problem, they just send you to the lawyer and the lawyer also does not want to listen.'

It is evident from examples such as these that employers must help their employees cope with circumstances and business requirements for which they often lack the necessary background or experience.

The Human Factor in Employment

Leading companies in South Africa have acknowledged the validity of establishing a sensitive employer-employee communications network and of taking cognisance of the human factor in the work situation. Crucial to the quality of work produced by an employee says Lawler (1970, p. 163) is the **job content.** 'Job content is the critical determinant of whether employees believe that good performance on the job leads to feelings of accomplishment, growth and self-esteem. That is, whether individuals will find jobs to be intrinsically motivating.' Lawler emphasises three characteristics which jobs must have to produce such results:

(a) the individual must receive meaningful feedback from his performance;
(b) he must be able to feel that he is using abilities he values for him to do the job effectively;
(c) he must feel he has a high degree of self-control in setting his own goals and defining the paths to these goals.

In other words, if the work situation is related to the individual meaningfully, the employee will release his optimum output and become committed and contented in his work. As Herzberg makes clear: 'Five factors stand out as strong determiners of job satisfaction – *achievement, recognition, work itself, responsibility* and *advancement*' – of which he stresses the last three in long-term planning. (1966, pp. 72–73)

In 1970 the New York State School of Industrial and Labour Relations found with regard to the work situation that 'both absenteeism and quit rates decline (without regard to sex) as employee salary and responsibility increases. But hours and other conditions of work are rarely conducive to responsible parenthood . . . so that compliance with work requirements often means relative neglect of home and family responsibilities.' (Howell, 1973, p. 254)

On the one hand then, personnel management is attempting to knit together the work and human elements to provide constant growth and individual stimulation and satisfaction. On the other, too little attention has as yet been given to what Erikson (1972, p. 33) calls 'relativity in human existence': ie that the individual must have 'a sense of coherent individuation and identity.' (p. 31) In other words not only will the job structure affect the individual and his relationships to those at home, but the home environment and its features must also be taken into account by those constructing the employment situation.

Weakness in the Employment Structure

In the context of present-day industrial theory and practice the case-studies reveal the need for certain improvements. As the case-studies of Brandt, Carlisle and Venter reveal, where the wage is inadequate the repercussions ripple often with serious negative consequences into the homes and lives of both the worker and his dependents. There is a need for equal pay for equal work and for upgrading the pay of people working at all levels of skill, **for it is often a woman machinist who is the actual breadwinner,** as Mrs Venter reveals.

Numerous economists have consistently expressed grave concern about the short and long-term national consequences of the system of job reservation. Professor Hobart Houghton sums up their arguments: 'Apart from any possible long-term political consequences arising from the frustration it engenders, the industrial colour bar has a number of immediate consequences which adversely affect national productivity. In so far as it prevents any man from performing a task for which he is competent, and confines him to one which is less skilled, there is economic waste of scarce resources ... In the denial of opportunities to non-whites, waste is incurred not only in the jobs they are precluded from performing, but also because of the effect this has upon their incentive to excel in the work they are permitted to perform.' (1964, p. 149) 'On the other side, the artificial protection afforded to some white workers tends also to lower efficiency because they lack the incentive afforded by healthy competition.' (p. 150) Hutt makes a further point, namely, that the system has 'caused the overcrowding and unjust cheapening of the occupations to which the non-whites have been confined'. (1964, p. 79)

Although the wage earned is the primary complaint in Western Township, the more educated are the ones most conscious of and frustrated by the colour bar. Ironically some people with University degrees or Librarianship Diplomas are doing clerical work because there are no openings for them in their vocation or because the pay in their first-choice situation is so much lower than their white counterparts that they are not prepared to endure the resultant relative privation.

There is a real need for professional skills to be rewarded and for manual work to be upgraded in status.

Not only is unemployment expensive to any society in terms of the morale of its people, as Mr Moss's case shows, but it adversely affects effective manpower utilisation. An unemployment agency in the Township is required through which both employers and prospective employees could advertise. This could be a mobile unit functioning in different townships on different days.

As the job turnover of people like Mrs Venter reveals, there is at present a need for employers to concern themselves:

(a) with the aspirations of their employees, and
(b) with induction and elucidating the job content and goals to the employee by means of job explanation and job training with a view to achieving job motivation and fulfilment.

Implementation of studies such as those of Lawler, Herzberg and others could receive more attention in this respect.

The example of Mrs de Kok indicates how perplexing bureaucracy can be to the less literate employee. We have seen how employers could greatly assist their workers by instructing them in the use of forms and conditions of work. Invaluable assets to people stemming from such an underprivileged environment would be lunch-time or work-time courses on aspects of life they find particularly problematical.

Employees like Mr Larson would feel more committed to their work if their requests for essentials such as protective clothing were met sincerely and promptly, indicating that the worker is indispensable to the company and valued as such.

Employers should constantly evaluate the job conditions they are offering, especially with regard to pay, hours of work, days a week, overtime, transport, and canteen feeding. Abramson and Gampel (1960, p. 1056) show what positive results have been achieved when employers have attended to matters such as better wages, food and the general health of workers. Other studies indicate how such measures ramify positively and influence the living habits of the worker's family.

The case-study of Mrs Mackenzie reveals that the position of the working mother, more so than the childless working wife, is a particularly delicate one both for her

and her employer. The problem is not confined to Western Township. 'Into every 24 hours the mother has to fit two jobs, one as mother, the other as an employee . . . She will be conscious of her dual loyalties, of home and work, and occasionally the conflicts that occur when responsibilities of one impinge on the other . . . The sick child at home – with difficulties of finding someone to nurse him constantly during the day – makes a day-long anxiety for the mother.' (Harris, 1970, p. 265)

Howell (1973, pp. 336-338) convincingly argues from the research of others that work per se need not negatively affect family life and the well-being of the children, if due consideration is given to the following factors in the mother's work:

(a) the job need be consonant with her skill and training and she need be rewarded (by recognition and promotion) for accomplishment. She adds that if these conditions are not met, her valuation of herself may be diminished not only in the employment situation but in her family relationships;

(b) she must not be forced into work against her will on account of finance;

(c) her husband must approve of her and lend support to her taking employment;

(d) satisfactory child-care arrangements must be provided, though these may be expensive and difficult to find.

A Holistic View of the Worker

From these findings it is clear that as far as possible employees must be viewed in terms of their **other social roles** for these will invariably affect work performances. All the above recommendations need to be considered with this in mind. Investment in crèches and pre-school centres at the industrial and governmental levels is a matter of urgency since nearly half the mothers in the Township work and their children as a result receive insufficient care and stimulation. We can no longer afford to have an industrial policy that works in vacuo, for it is the quality of life in the society in which the worker operates that influences his behaviour and ultimately how he works.

Industry can increasingly play a part in a Township such as Western by providing educational benefits such as school buildings, cultural facilities, training centres or study bursaries, so relating work incentives to the employee's background and investing in a new generation of more literate workers in consultation with the people themselves.

The previously-mentioned housing programmes and related projects such as health services could be provided by industry and government through mutual liaison committees; such would positively affect the worker's productivity and his sense of industrial belonging which in turn should increase the possibilities of betterment of his peripheral relationships. At times when the home situation is complex, as in the Venter case, it will be necessary for industry, the Department of Social Welfare and the family concerned to work out a joint programme of rehabilitative action.

It is thus evident that labour policies affecting employees such as those of Western Township need to relate to the environmental situation from which the worker emerges. Employees value a considerate and understanding employer and this is a necessary precondition to sound working relations. In addition employers need to concentrate their energies on relating the individual employee to the organisation, and to break down areas of misunderstanding and poor communication between the two.

There is a need not only for short-term ameliorative action as suggested above, but for longer-term basic structural changes in the employment situation. Government, industry, and the Coloured Representative Council need prepare the way for meaningful worker participation and allow responsible collective bargaining in employment, without which, as the present circumstances indicate, the worker's voice goes unheeded.

Only once the work factor is positively interrelated with that of the home environment and the needs of the worker can we expect to find the men and women of Western Township becoming fully productive.

FOOTNOTES

1. The Minimum Effective (Household) Level computed for a Coloured family of five living in Johannesburg during the same period is R165,44. (Potgieter, J. F. 1974. *Research Report No. 14,* Institute for Planning Research, University of Port Elizabeth.)
2. The term is somewhat arbitrary since class division is by no means as distinct as in Britain, for example.
3. Four months later I found her in hospital. She had collapsed from lack of food.
4. The figure at the time, but the amount has increased (February 1975) as the following table shows:

	White	*Coloured*	*African*	
Maximum pension:	R57,00	29,50	11,25	(per person, per month).

Chapter 7
Alcoholism

To analyse why certain people consume alcohol to the point of excess and addiction it is first necessary to understand what psychophysiological changes alcohol consumption induces in man. Alcohol is a depressant which acts as a stimulant. People who do not drink socially, drink for the **effect** which liquor has on them. To these people, alcohol is a liberator: it temporarily removes the pain of human existence and makes life more tolerable. The dividing line between the heavy drinker and the alcoholic is a narrow one, but it hinges on this difference, that an alcoholic is addicted to liquor to the extent that he can no longer exist without it.

Theories regarding the Causes of Alcoholism

Some of the most tenable theories of alcoholism explain the phenomenon in psychosocial or cultural terms. Thus Bales (1946, p. 482) and others[1] relate the degree of alcoholism in society to the extent that the society does not resolve the subsistence anxieties and life insecurities of its members.

Park (1962, p. 452) emphasises that it is 'drinking to relieve particular types of tensions arising from particular types of social situations that leads to alcoholism' and Rip (1964, p. 247)[2] speaks of relative deprivation ie the 'person feels that, relative to satisfactions obtained by others, whom he uses as a reference group or reference person, he has been deprived'.

Ullman on the other hand deduces that where there is cultural equivocation towards drinking, ie some people approve the habit whilst others demur (eg the conflicting morality of the Anglo-Saxon Americans) there is likely to be a high rate of alcoholism.[3]

Drinking goals are also important. If a people's drinking patterns are symbolically associated with social or religious communication as with the American Jews, there is usually a low rate of inebriety; but if the main reason for drinking is pleasure and for the **effect** alcohol has on people, as amongst the American Irish, a high rate of alcoholism will usually prevail. This means that persons who drink for the effects which alcohol produces in them are likely to drink excessively; they will tend to prefer distilled liquors, eg Cane Spirits, for their alcohol content or proof is related to the immediacy and degree with which the desired results are achieved; they will have little need to show moderation in drinking because restraint has no relation to their goal; and they are more likely to become dependent on alcohol to solve personal problems. (Glad, 1947, pp. 452-6, 461-2)

The National Council on Alcoholism in New York suggests that the following factors are likely to point to High Risk Persons: a family and kin history of alcoholism; a family history of teetotalism especially if associated with strong moral overtones and if the person now moves in a drinking social environment; descendant of a broken home; one characterised by parental discord, or an absent or rejecting father; and female kin of more than one generation with a high degree of recurrent depressions. (Criteria Committee, 1972, p. 257)

Various early life influences also have a bearing on later alcoholism. Seventy three percent of the alcoholics the McCords studied (1960, p. 71) came from families manifesting at least one of the following behaviour patterns: maternal alternation between showing love and rejection; maternal escapism; antagonistic relationship between the parents; deviancy – criminal, promiscuous or alcoholic behaviour of the mother; denigration of the mother by the father; maternal resentment of her role in the family.

They found furthermore that alcoholics rejected their paternal models and had few clearly expressed intentions imposed on them, these factors leading to a distorted image of self. Most had experienced general stress, erratic satisfaction of their dependency needs and conflict over a heightened desire for such. A clear specific image of manhood was not projected by the father, thus an alternative masculine image would be sought.

The Importance of Role Relatedness

These are some of the most valuable approaches to alcoholism produced by theorists. They deal primarily with social roles and mutual relationships in society, and indicate that in societies of the western world alcoholism is primarily a **male** disorder. Traditionally, woman has had a more clearly defined and manageable role as wife and mother with little visible failure accompanying it. The man however has had to contend with the multiple pressures of being the breadwinner. This means that he 'can fail not only in his familial but also in his occupational role; the possibility that a man's self-image will be publicly deflated is greater.' (McCords, 1960, p. 163)

The theories further indicate that it is not only important for a human being to understand and be able to tolerate the laws and customs of his sub or total-culture but that **he must subconsciously feel related to its parts and the whole in a meaningful way,** and at the same time have access to intrinsic and real fulfilment mechanisms so as to feel emotionally whole.

It has become fashionable to decry anxiety and frustration as related causes of alcoholism. This may be because they have too often been unspecific blanket terms of little utilitarian value. However it is obvious that if a person underachieves in life, whether it be the executive who cannot attain promotion or a husband who cannot find the right outlet for his aptitudes socially or adjust to familial demands, he will be undergoing stress. In order to prevent him finding detrimental stress-outlets, it is necessary to analyse what roles and clusters build up most anxiety for him, and to devise methods of defusing their effect. We need to relate the individual to the various social circles in which he revolves or which influence his life directly and indirectly. In short, we need to come to terms with the problems of human adjustment.[4]

Causes of Alcoholism in Western Township

The following factors relate to alcoholism in Western Township.

(a) The need for companionship

Western Township is a conglomeration of people who have been officially moved from some other area in Johannesburg or who have come to Johannesburg from rural areas and diverse parts of the country. They differ from the 'Cape Coloureds' in that they have little common background or feeling of kinship with the people around them.

Some say how difficult it is to accustom themselves to town life '*en al die pampiere*' ('and all the papers') the most striking example being that of a Hottentot lady in her twenties whose home had always been the Kalahari and whose food was '*springbok vleis en wortels, omdat niks daar groei nie.*' ('springbok meat and wild roots – because nothing grows there.') She went to work for some whites when food became too scarce and moved with them to Johannesburg. She is married to an African man by whom she has a child but finds it hard to learn Afrikaans, to cook and eat town food, dress and live so differently from what she has been accustomed to. Although most Coloured people do not experience such a dramatic cultural shock, nevertheless even when they have moved voluntarily they find the uprooting plunges them into a world of isolation lacking in socio-cultural buffers, and most inhabitants show distinct signs of loneliness and lostness with a tendency to withdraw into themselves.

One of the main ways of becoming part of a group and making friends is by accepting a drink. Once the initial step has been taken, although it may merely have been for reasons of sociability, the round of drinks, parties with friends, or drinking as a means of making human contact tends to generate a pattern of increased drinking.

Such a situation is similar to that discussed by Ullman, namely that: 'It is not at all unusual to find someone who having been moved from his customary residence to an isolated group such as an army camp, lumber camp or foreign resort . . . drinks less temperately than at home . . . Removal from one's typical way of life may involve deprivations and usually does mean some anxiety. In these unusual circumstances, alcohol is useful in reducing anxiety.' (1958, p. 54)

(b) Ambivalence within the culture

As in the Cape Town study of Gillis et al (1973) approximately 70% of the women of Western Township are complete abstainers. Coloured women are at the same time renowned for their intense religious fervour. They usually regard drinking as 'bad' or 'wrong' for religious reasons or abstain because of the heavy drinking of the men and 'if two of you drink, who will look after the children?'

A high degree of abstinence in women in Western and a high degree of drinking and alcoholism amongst men bode ill for the younger generation, because 'High ambivalence towards the use of alcohol can also be created in the child by the parents having **conflicting** drinking patterns even where they belong to the same language group . . . in fact where there are different drinking patterns and attitudes towards drink from which a person must choose, then one can expect ambivalence, and where ambivalence is found, there alcoholism can be expected because of the tension and frustration resulting.' (Rip, 1964, p. 47)

The child of an alcoholic may find himself in a position in which he has first-hand experience of the negative consequences of alcoholism yet simultaneously finds himself under a compulsion to drink. This absence of a common standard of values with regard to alcohol also affects the present adult generation because it leads to tensions and conflicts between family and friends.

(c) Drinking for its effect

There is the widespread viewpoint that drinking has always been a form of leisure for Coloured people, originally associated with repayment for labour on the farms. The 'tot system' was considered part-payment for labour. In most cases it meant . . . 'giving the labourers six tots of wine per day – two before breakfast . . . two before lunch . . . a fifth in the afternoon, and the sixth on stopping work'. (Ziervogel, nd p. 38)

The men in Western often illustrate that when they drink they like to pour a bottle of wine down their throats until their bodies begin to sag backwards and their heads rest against a wall and the world fades into a haze. Many people say they turn to drink as a means of respite from life's hardships. This is confirmed by Professor Erika Theron's study where she observes that: 'Although the use of alcohol leads to serious impoverishment and ill health (especially tuberculosis) amongst the Coloureds, their poor economic conditions, inadequate housing, and lack of opportunities socially for realising their ambitions, also lead to abuse of alcohol.

Many of the Coloureds drink to escape from poverty and restriction to a world of fantasy which offers a temporary release from harsh reality.' (1955, pp. 40–41)[5]

(d) Socio-economic conditions

Western Township has the characteristic slum features of shabby inadequate dwellings, deprivation and crime. As one man expostulated in anger: 'I loathe this Township, there's not a thing about it that I like.'

A lack of community feeling is a part of the aggression-frustration-insecurity syndrome which plagues the inhabitants. Most of the people hate the Township, its conditions, and its way of life, in particular the terror-wielding teenage gangs, the oppressive houses and their perpetual inability as adults to eat, sleep, visit, clean, wash and relax in two or three small rooms. As a result parents become irritable: the children being so much in their way.

The socio-economic position of the men is a significant contributory cause of alcoholism, closely allied to the political structure which has as yet failed to give them a positive sense of identity. (cf. chapter 8)

(e) Lack of artistic outlets

There are some highly sensitive and intelligent people living in Western Township who crave meaningful artistic outlets but cannot find them and so often turn to drink. 'How shall I put it, the person like me who loves drama, or dining in a nice restaurant, or music, or reading books – not the sort of books which they choose for us in this Library, we want to select our own books – for this type of person there is nothing in life. A person is not a robot, he can't just go to work every day of his life and return, sleep, and tomorrow the same and always the same. A person has a soul and the soul must also be fulfilled and grow and be fed, for you are not a machine. They do nothing for our soul, and if our people's soul starves, then we begin to drink.'

(f) Poverty

Some people drink because they are poor. A man's income can't meet the cost of living: 'I can't earn enough to support my children decently and I'm behind in my death insurance and burial is expensive in Johannesburg – this worries me day and night.' (He earns R40 a month.)

Everyday the man comes home to the same problems of overcrowding, needy children and a struggling wife: there is little to uplift him. As Kerrin points out: 'The more fortunate individual need only drink until his immediate surroundings take on a rosier hue, but for the slum dweller this is impossible. The same amount of drink only makes his immediate surroundings more hateful than ever. He must go on drinking until his squalid environment fades out entirely.' 'If a man leaves his daily work not for the rest and relaxation of a comfortable home but for the dirt and squalor of an overcrowded slum, a moderate amount of alcohol is worse than useless. It relaxes inhibitions just as it does in the case of the more fortunate individual, but in this case the relaxation takes place precisely in conditions where greater and not less self-control is required. The conflicting needs of people who are compelled to live in crowded slums demand an impossibly high standard of morality if they are to live together in peace and amity,' (1945, p. 12) and this can only be achieved by a constant succession of sacrifices by every household member. Researchers commonly relate alcoholism and drug abuse amongst the lower classes to social conditions which promote despair and apathy as an inexpensive escape from an unbearable reality. Thus Freud (1948, p. 402) remarked: 'We shall probably discover that the poor are even less ready to part with their neuroses than the rich, because the hard life that awaits them when they recover has no attraction.'

(g) Men deprived of masculinity

Conditions at home and work are not divorced from one another for both impinge on the psyche of the male ego. Many Coloured men in the Township express their frustration at job reservation: though in many cases they have equal abilities to their white counterparts they are still not allowed to take certain jobs or to earn the same wage. This resentment at not receiving recognition and not being given responsibility according to their aptitudes turns some men to drink. Others will say that after a day's work they are so emotionally outraged at having to submit to white paternalism that when they return home to an 'overcrowded house and this lousy township – I just can't stand it,' and they go and have a drink.

The psychological effect is thus seen in the Coloured man losing his sense of worth and seeking to escape from this reality through drink. In Western Township men of all earning powers manifest this sense of inadequacy and diminished self-respect and a tendency towards a complete discarding of any responsibility in personal, familial or societal matters. It is evident that the lives of the people in Western manifest the same tendencies as Steyn found in the West Cape[6] and Gillis and others (1973, p. 1381) in Cape Town. 'There has always been a great deal of dependence among the Coloured population, economically and in terms of authority, upon external persons or agencies – employers, farmers, the police, housing managers, and so on. This type of society can be highly supportive to people until they find themselves involved in an individualised, competitive, urban, industrial society. Many persons in the lower classes, particularly recent migrants, are just not adept at handling this sort of individual responsibility, and repercussions follow. The men, particularly in poverty-stricken or socially disorganised families, bear less responsibility for the status and maintenance of their dependants than in the middle-class families, and as a consequence the women take on a more important providing and arranging role, for the safeguarding of the children is the ultimate necessity and an important factor in keeping the family together . . . All in all, therefore, lower-class males tend to bear a diminished responsibility and status in the family and this has a lot to do with the excessive drinking among them because, after having contributed perfunctorily as breadwinners, they may get drunk without being held to account too stringently.'

(h) The need for an acknowledged identity

It thus becomes evident that beneath all the other irritations which upset the balance of the Coloured person in general and the male in particular there is a root malady, and that is **a crisis of identity.** A feature of the world's racially dissected societies is the profound insecurity experienced by minority groups, especially those which do not fit into the established social pattern. In common with such people the quandary of the average Coloured person in Western Township is his consequent uncertainty as to who he is and where he belongs in South African society. His behaviour shows the ambivalence he senses in white attitudes and legislation towards him until in the end he also rejects himself.

This was vividly exemplified in the interview I had with Samuel, a man in his late fifties addicted to Methylated Spirits and known in the Township as one of the 'Spirits People'.[7] He was grovelling on a filthy kitchen floor yelling obscenities. His middle-aged sister would either ignore him or shout in disgust: 'Agh shut up,' to which he would endlessly yell: 'Shut up, you fucking bastard!' while the children sat quiet and tense in the adjacent room.

His sister would say: 'He does nothing except drink, swear and roll around on the floor every day. It's driving me mad!' At that stage he staggered up to me and aggressively asked if I believed her. A stream of mucus shot out of his nose, whereupon he took a child's dress near him to wipe it off, politely saying: 'Excuse me.' His actions and speech were the slow repetitive gestures of the alcoholic. At this point his sister stormed off her chair and hurtled towards him shouting: *'Laat los, laat los!'* ('Let go, let go!') I watched in confusion as she screamed at him: *'Laat los my wasgoed.'* ('Leave my washing.') 'You're not cleaning your nose on my clean washing!' whereupon he stormed past me and shouted: 'Shut up, fuck off . . . shut up!' She pulled the dress away and the shouting and action became tenser as she tore off a dirty piece of newspaper from the floor and told him to wipe his nose with that: 'That's fit for you, not the clean washing.' When the outburst subsided momentarily I directed the conversation to the man.

He said he had been drinking for a long time and couldn't stop now because *'what is there to live for?'* He had been a driver and feels he should now be able to relax a little and do nothing. He drinks at a shebeen with friends a few houses away and also at home when his sister doesn't pour the Methylated Spirits out of the window. He also buys Methylated Spirits at the store. His sister walked out as he began to wax eloquent, prefacing every sentence with *'Mevrou, of is dit nou Juffrou'* ('Mrs, or is it now Miss') until in the end he pulled a chair up and said: 'Miriam. You're an intelligent woman. You talk sense. You tell me what to do . . . I want to get out of here. I hate the place . . . everyone is terrible to me, nobody speaks to me . . . Miriam you must help me! Now tell me what to do.'

Suddenly when we were talking he stood up, slapped me heartily on the back and jubilantly pronounced: 'You know Miriam. I must thank you very much Miriam. Very, very much Miriam.' 'Oh? for what?' 'You know Miriam I must thank you. You have done a wonderful thing. **You have spoken to me today,** Miriam. Miriam I don't remember anyone talking to me like that.' I tried to pass this off as a joke but he called a friend from outside and continued: 'Miriam you have done a great thing today. I will never forget this day Miriam. I will never forget this thing.' And then he turned to his friend proudly and said: *'Sien hoe sy praat met my!'* ('Look how she talks with me!')

People need to be recognised and to feel a sense of individual worth. Loss of this can be critically debilitating.

Treating the Symptoms of Alcoholism

To date, official concern with alcoholism in the Township has been restricted to allowing SANCA, a registered welfare organisation, to work with people who voluntarily wish to be cured, and periodic police raids on the shebeens in the community.

But such operations are unrealistic in treating the causes of the problem. Cognisance needs to be taken of **why** people drink. A campaign within the Township levelled at educating the community on the dangers of alcohol need be organised; and consideration must be taken of the fact that if shebeens did not operate, people would still be able to get as much liquor from bottle-stores inside and outside the Township and in the municipal bar lounges in the adjacent township of Newclare.

The Shebeen in Western Township

It is, I believe, incorrect to blame the shebeens in the Township for the high rate of drunkenness and alcoholism in the community or to stigmatise them as vice-dens. There are important factors concerning them that are generally overlooked.

Most people who frequent shebeens do so because they enjoy the companionship of others and the convivial atmosphere. Here they are welcomed, fussed over and cared for in a way that is usually not forthcoming in a struggling routine-bound home.[8]

It is wrong to generalise about shebeens. They vary in the quality and type of service they offer. Just as in the retail world, some do good business on sound principles, make excellent profits and live well by the trade, others just manage to exist from their earnings and still others remain extremely poor.

There are certain shebeens which would prefer to be called 'Pub-Houses' – high-class, electrically-lit, spacious converted homes with all the modern conveniences wherein the owner spends time, money and initiative in improving and transforming a hovel into an inviting place of relaxation. Such an owner will accommodate in one place those men and women who prefer to drink separately, and in another those who like to drink together. He will select his clients and turn away those he feels might 'roughen up' the atmosphere. He does not allow the very young to drink and works strictly for cash. This type of liquor establishment does not sell 'Bantu Beer' but only the higher status beer out of bottles, and many of his clients prefer spirits. One owner remarked that he felt white people had better drinking habits than Coloured people: 'A white man can have a glass or two to drink but keeps a bottle of gin for a week, but the Coloured, he wants to finish the bottle at one go.'[9]

Another owner aims at getting all his children well-educated and is giving them the best possible schooling opportunities, together with ballet and drama lessons. What is especially noteworthy at such pub-houses is that the owners' children are invariably **not** found in the streets or in gangs but even at eight years old are aiming to be doctors and lawyers! **One receives the impression that these people are striving to improve their economic and social position in life and that of their children – though in an unorthodox and illegal manner.**

At the other extreme there are shebeens which sell mainly 'Bantu Beer' and cheap '*White Malmsey*' (White Wine) and powerful home brews such as 'Barberton' – though the penalties for these brews are so severe that they are becoming rare. Here there is often overcrowding, lack of hygiene, unpleasantness and fighting, especially if frequented by one of the gangs. 'Sometimes a gang of *tsotsis* comes for a drink and then refuses to pay.' Most of these shebeens work on pay-day credit systems and people are then free to drink on the deposit they have laid down. Only in a few cases do they develop into brothels.

Then there are others who try to patch up their homes to make them more inviting and sell the favoured drinks, White Wine, Brandy, Sherry, Cane Spirits and Beer (bottled and Bantu) in a respectable manner. Two such sisters were unemployed and therefore entered into this business: '*want 'n mens moet iets doen om 'n bietjie geld te kry*' ('because a person has to do something to earn a little money.') The one sister however hates drunkards and says she can only tolerate them by drinking a little herself.

Because shebeens are officially outlawed they subject themselves to considerable expense in operating a security network against the police; in addition they are not subject to any ruling on selling prices, so their drinks are expensive. For there is of course a host of associates who have to be paid in liquor or cash for services rendered: the little children who act as unofficial scouts, the gang or adult men attached as watchers and deflectors of 'the law', those who ensure by violent or other means that trouble-makers or debtors mend their ways, the women or men who store the liquor at their houses lest the shebeen is raided, or even certain policemen who allegedly will accept bribes or 'free' drinks at certain shebeens in exchange for timely warnings of raids. Thus a skilful and quite effective counter-attack network has evolved extending the successful running of a shebeen beyond the activity of the owner alone and uniting numerous people of all ages who develop some form of vested interest in the place plus a dislike for the police.

Some shebeen owners regret that much of their time, energy and sometimes money is spent '*met die sake by die Hof*' ('with matters at the Court') – though even here certain tactical measures are resorted to. Most shebeens have an atmosphere of insecurity and quiet caution as a result of intermittent police raids. Owners of shebeens, whether men or women, say that one never gets used to police raids and when one is caught *'dan is almal net stil in die huis en hul treur dat jy kan dink daar is 'n dood hier'* ('then everyone is just quiet in the house and they mourn so that you think there is a death here.')

Although some Coloured people, especially mothers, say that shebeen owners have no real moral conscience and are evil, not everyone believes this and there is a good deal of legitimacy in the emphatic denial by shebeen owners who explain that **the people come to the shebeen of their own accord; the shebeen does not advertise or go to the people:** 'I do not go out and call the people to my shebeen; the people come to me.'

Shebeen owners do not consider themselves to be any different **in practice** from white bottle-stores or pubs (except that they may be a bit more expensive since they have to buy their liquor from them). They say there are many shops in Johannesburg that are allowed to sell people things even if they are harmful to health, for example cigarettes, sweets and alcohol, and white people do not hold such retailers responsible for the moral or physical wellbeing of the community – it's the community's voluntary choice to spend money in a certain way at a certain place. 'If you sell anything in a shop, it's not the shopkeeper's fault if you choose to buy it.'

Shebeen and pub-owners also disagree that they are the cause of family break-ups for they find that there is usually a problem in those households anyway.

In the context of Western Township, the person who runs a drinking-house appears as just one of many people who has to devise a way of earning a living. Some go into the business because it appears lucrative, others because they can't find a job or the right kind of job in the white sector.

The whole concept of illegality thus appears anachronistic, for apart from Health Visitors looking after infants and the occasional social worker, the only other people concerned with the Township seem to be the rent collectors and the police. The people feel that neither whites nor the Coloured Affairs Department care about Western, so its people develop their own modus vivendi. In consequence the pouncing of the police on certain shebeens or the swoop of the vice-squad on people found gambling, hits the Township like some hated hurricane. And because negative contacts are the only real contacts with the law-makers of the country, it is small wonder that public opinion in the Township is so reluctant to uphold the law.

Pinpointing the Real Causes of Alcoholism

Thus although it is true that too much money is being spent on liquor by many Coloured adults in Western, and this is one of the contributory reasons for underfed children, perpetuation of the poverty cycle, and marital disharmony, yet the shebeen is not the cause of the high level of drunkenness and alcoholism, it is merely one of the means towards it.

A Municipal Worker in Western Township once said to me: 'The trouble with these Coloureds is they drink too much . . . Man, and the funny thing is that the poorer they are the more they drink.' A social worker who works in the Township sighs and says: 'This place just leads to depression,' whilst Health Visitors and people who work with the alcoholics say: 'The best thing to do is to bulldoze the whole place down and start again.' Their despair is due to their attempt at curing malnourished children or alcoholics and then sending them back into the identical social environment of poverty and helplessness which caused the malaise in the first place.

The Cost to South Africa

South Africa today has one of the highest alcoholism rates in the world, of which Coloured males are amongst the main victims.[10] Drinking is regarded as a pleasurable asset related to the leisure and even work of all population groups in the country as is seen from the fact that R584 million was spent on alcohol in 1973.[11] Louw (1974, p. 78) quotes Coombes' finding that the total cost of untreated alcoholism to South African employers according to the 1970 population census was as follows:

Cost of untreated alcoholism to South African employers in 1970

Cost to:	
Coloured employers	R40 844 160
White employers	R65 440 000
Total:	R106 284 160
Add: Pre-addictive but problem drinkers	R30 000 000
Grand total:	R136 284 160

Alcoholism is costing South Africa too much in terms of individual, family and economic stability for us to continue to rely on short-staffed charitable organisations and punitive police measures to try to cope with it. Rather we must seek to tackle the **multiple negative influences** that cause tensions and conflicts within the community.

Recommendations concerning Alcoholism

The suggestions which follow are intended as possible stepping-stones towards the eradication of alcoholism in Western Township. Only such as are specifically related to alcoholism are dealt with here, the more general recommendations being dealt with in the final chapter (see pp. 79-85).

The Department of Social Welfare needs to establish depots in areas of acute drunkenness and alcoholism to assist SANCA in curative work. (At present follow-up treatment is virtually impossible through lack of staff and inpatient units.) The use of volunteers is especially encouraged.

Relevant community programmes should be actively pursued by the Coloured Affairs Department, Coloured Representative Council and local inhabitants with leadership qualities, to encourage people to develop creative outlets, thus helping to provide meaningful substitutes for drinking.

Education on the use and abuse of alcohol should become part of the school curriculum and lectures on the problem should be arranged at places of employment.

Liquor advertisements should be made subject to certain restrictions with regard to misleading claims.

An impartial investigation needs to be conducted into the position of the shebeens with a view to the possibility of legalising them. Not only could this bring into the open what could be a legitimate occupation, but a system of appropriate licences and liaison with the owners could be created. It would also remove a very real area of insecurity, tension and hostility to the law.

FOOTNOTES

1. See Horton, 1943, p. 297; Haer, 1955, p. 184.
2. Following Stauffer.
3. Compare Reader's summary of findings, 1964, p. 204.

4. Cf. Mowrer, H. R. & E. R. 1945, p. 37.
5. Translated from the Afrikaans.
6. In Cilliers, 1964, pp. 106–125.
7. ie People addicted to Meths.
8. The situation is similar to the saloons which developed in England and the United States after the Industrial Revolution. Sociologists have noted how such public houses helped to overcome the emotional strain of monotony, poverty and loneliness in the city. As Moore wrote of the Chicago saloon to which the working man went: "Many of his leisure hours are spent here. In it he finds more of the things which approximate to luxury than he finds at home, almost more than he finds in any other public place in the ward . . . But his demand for even these things is not fundamental; they are but the means to his social expression. It is the society of his fellows that he seeks and must have." (1897, pp. 4–5)
9. It is worth noting that Coloured men prefer distilled beverages. Their orientation thus characterises them as a people using alcohol for *affective* reasons (cf. Glad, pp. 452–453). Such usage is related to a high incidence of alcoholism.
10. This has been confirmed by SANCA but accurate figures are unavailable.
11. Johannesburg, *The Star*, 2. 11. 1974.

Chapter 8
Identity

In the late 1950's when the African people were officially moved out of Western Native Township and Sophiatown, Coloured people were moved into the area. It was renamed 'Western Coloured Township' (now 'Western Township') and the Coloured inhabitants were promised that the crumbling rented houses were a temporary stop-gap whilst new dwellings were built and reconstruction was in progress.

The Negative Character of the Township

In 1961 there were 2 000 houses in Western Township. They were in a poor state of repair and lacking in essential home conveniences such as ceilings, electricity, hot or indoor water and baths. But over the succeeding 10 years little has been done to improve the situation, the dwellings have deteriorated still further (many leak and are damp) and only 500 units have been demolished in the area. Thus in 1975 1 500 of the original dwellings remain.

The area has gradually disintegrated into an amorphous group of people characterised by neglect, indigence, gang warfare, marital violence, alcoholism, illegitimacy and a lack of community feeling.

Outsiders look down on the Township because it is poor or violent, whilst Coloured people in neighbouring areas tend to consider themselves distinctly superior to their fellows here: 'We're not like the Western's, they're only Kaffirs.' Even Coloured High School teachers who educate some of the children from this Township are adamant in their stereotypes: 'Oh Western, they are the "sun-sitters", they loaf and sit in the sun all day. They don't want work, they gamble enough to pay their low rent and the shebeens – that's all they want.' Very seldom does one meet with any understanding of and concern for the people, though the occasional person will say: '*Western – nou dis 'n treurige plek*' ('Western – now that's a sad place.')

Although there are inhabitants of Western who do not mind living in the Township as they do not mix with other people and '*ek is nou gewoond aan die plek – 'n mens moet maar jouself aanpas*' ('I am now used to the place – after all a person must adjust') most people fear and dislike it because it is so rough. One frequently hears statements such as: 'I've never seen people live like this – they kill on a Friday in broad daylight!' or 'Western is terribly rough. Where I grew up life wasn't like this. Here they kill each other and throw stones on your roof – you can't feel safe.'

On questioning local people as to why they felt Western had so many negative features one interesting theory emerged: 'The place is cursed so it won't get right.' Someone else explained this belief: '*Toe die Bantoe hier gewoon het wou hulle nie weg van die plek gaan nie, hulle het baie van die Western gehou. Toe forseer die Regering dat hulle na Soweto moet trek. Toe hulle trek het die Bantoe 'n vloek hier gelos want die Bantoe was baie hartseer om hier weggaan.*' ('When the Bantu lived here they did not want to leave the place, they were very attached to this Western. Then the Government forced them to move to Soweto. When they moved the Bantu left a curse here because the Bantu were very heartsore to leave.')

Invariably one hears people say how nice Western was when in its early years the Africans were still living there. 'Then I would come home from work in the early evening and they would be sitting on their verandahs and they were quiet and friendly, and people would walk about visiting at night. The young men didn't worry you. But when they gradually had to leave and the Coloureds came in it all changed.' Quite a number of the inhabitants had also lived in Sophiatown and although it was poverty-stricken, rough and squalid, maintained that it had vitality and exuberance: 'It sparkled with life.' Most people say: 'It was nicer than here,' and the general sentiment is: 'The Africans are very bright people. Sophiatown had character and life and colour. Alcohol is all we Coloureds have.'[1]

People tend to feel that not only has Western deteriorated until it has reached a stage where 'a person can't rear a child properly because the atmosphere here is so bad,' but also that the problems of Western are a consequence of the fact that: 'the Coloureds are given very little.'

To some extent the absence of community feeling in Western Township reminds one of similar problems reported by Jennings on Barton Hill (east of Bristol, UK), viz that every area has a history of difficulties and unfriendliness and that the development of community spirit emerges from this very slowly. Gavron indicates how 'working-class' people are at a particular disadvantage when moved to a new place, for she found it is the middle-class who 'have learned the necessary verbal and social skills required in getting to know new people' (1970, p. 104) and that this equips them more adequately to be neighbourly. At the same time one feels that such difficulties are aggravated in Western Township through weak departmental organisation and a lack of commitment by those responsible for its development.

Thus we not only need to take positive steps to improve the physical environment, but we must be wary of moving tenants too often. In addition, as the British studies show, housing officers must analyse and set in motion a programme for aiding the tenants' **psychological** adjustment to new conditions and assisting them in developing feelings of neighbourliness and a sense of belonging.

Lack of Facilities

Although the authorities have established a number of playing fields, the people of Western do not regard themselves as having sufficient outlets for recreation. One of the most striking deterrents is their terror of the panga gangs and the feeling that the police and relevant authorities are not making efforts to break these up.

Van der Ross emphasises the effect of a lack of personal safety on the Coloured person: 'It brings about a deplorable mental attitude . . . of acceptance and resignation to a situation of which the individual does not approve, but which he feels to be too big for him. He therefore either succumbs to it or withdraws entirely into his home after dark; in either case he deprives both himself and his family of much of the normal home life to which they are entitled.' (1971, p. 12)

Others complain that the two cinemas in neighbouring Newclare show 'rubbish, violence and sex', and when they read of an educative or cultural film which interests them showing in Johannesburg they cannot go to it because it is for Whites.

Finally there are people like a group of young intellectuals who tried to initiate poetry reading evenings but found that after one month no-one seemed interested. Only the executive was left and it was disbanded. The inhabitants seem to have fallen into a state of lethargy for reasons I shall elucidate later.

The Housing Problem

Perhaps the most potentially explosive issue in the Township is housing.[2] Ten thousand people of Western are still living in the sub-standard housing they were promised was a **temporary** measure 12 years ago. By now some families have already grown up there and the damage is done; in other cases husband and wife lodge in one place, their children board with the granny in another; then there are those who although they don't get on have to share a house with in-laws. Others are frustrated because there are no mental homes for Coloured people and they are obliged to have mentally disturbed people and alcoholics living with them in their cramped conditions. Such stories can be multiplied. Only the really destitute are satisfied with nothing but a roof over their heads. Generally the houses are too small. One mother of eight children explains: 'Look we have just two rooms and you clean all the time and it doesn't improve, because there is only one door and everyone walks over the same ground and bumps things – and this is where you sleep and make fire, and wash and make food and do everything, it's very difficult.'

Another mother, Jane, and her husband, desperate for a house, were living with her aunt and her family. She has been married for four years and has been on the waiting list for three. Her children live with her mother-in-law elsewhere in the Township. Her mother-in-law made Jane's life such a misery that she left her for '*sy is nie lief vir mense, jy kan nie in so 'n huis woon*' ('she's not fond of people, you can't live in such a house.') Nevertheless she says the mother-in-law is very fond of the children and treats them well; but as a **family** they simply can't continue with a normal family or marital life. Her husband works very hard and earns R40 a week as a driver for a waste-removal firm; sometimes with overtime he can earn up to R90 a week. She has been to the Council nearly every week and they keep promising her a house. She knows other people have applied for a house later than she has and have got one. Now she has told her husband that they will just have to forfeit R100 if it means they will get a house by some underhand method.

Numerous people say they have been on the waiting list for a new house for 12 years and yet newcomers come in and get a flat or row-house 'in no time'. They are convinced there is much bribery and feel the Coloured officials are worse than the whites.[3] One morning I was talking with three women sitting on upturned boxes on the cold concrete floor of a tiny room with the paint peeling off the walls, when one of them jumped up, looked through the window and exclaimed: 'Ooh, look at that smooth rent officer, now where's he going to make trouble? I tell you I would have no conscience in trying to cheat him. Because he's a Coloured man, he earns R200 a month and gets a cheap R18 a month flat. I like that! Ag, they all just suit themselves and take the bribes.'

The people feel frustrated because their complaints never seem to receive a sympathetic hearing: 'All they ever say to us is: "I don't give you a house for your furniture," or: "You shouldn't have so many children then you wouldn't be cramped!"' They feel resentful that 'you get no choice of the house you want to move into; they just inform you that you are going to move. And if you want to add a room onto the house, you pay for it but the Council has its own ideas about what you can build on.' Others who detest the cramped conditions say: 'I'm not an animal, I can't live like this.' Such people have lost interest in Western and the environment and say 'all I want to do is get out of Western'.

High Rentals

Those people with a sufficiently high income are disgruntled because of the exorbitant rents they have to pay in relation to their income. The rent varies from R6-R8 a month in the old area, but in the redeveloped area people who are earning R180 a month and have five children are paying R48 a month in rent, excluding electricity. I was frequently asked: 'Have you seen the new flats they have built for the whites on the other side of Newlands? They are paying R18[4] a month and the flats are much better quality, but no, '*ons kan dit nie vir die Kleurlinge doen nie*' ('we can't do that for the Coloureds').

A new sub-economic row-house area is being built, for which people can apply if they have a maximum income of R80 a month, but people are chary about the whole scheme. A certain section is also planned to house pensioners, but the minimum rent is R11 a month and their pension is R29,50 a month. In addition to this people complain that their electricity bills average R8 a month, thus leaving them with R10,50 per month for food, clothing and any transport or items of comfort.

This is indicated by the following tables:

Economic flats and row-houses: Westbury Ext 2

Type of unit	*Rental per month*		
	R81-R130	R131-R320	R321-Over[5]
90 Three-bedroom Row Houses	R35,40	R51,40	R55,35
28 Four-bedroom Row Houses	R40,25	R58,60	R63,10
132 One-bedroom flats	R27,80	R39,55	R42,45
144 Two-bedroom flats	R31,95	R45,55	R48,95

124 Sub-economic dwellings: Westbury Ext 2

Type of unit	*Rental per month*		
	R0-R80	R81-R130	R131+
52 Four-Room Semi-detached Houses	R13,05	R18,85	R26,10
24 Two-Room Flats	R11,00	R15,95	R22,15
48 Flatlets for Old Age Pensioners[6]	R11,00	R15,95	R22,15

Increasingly the people of Western are becoming suspicious of the Government's intentions towards them: 'Now look, they're building these row-houses here: sub-economic! They just want to push us under and move the scum in here from up there [the old area]. We don't want to live with them – all those low-down people. And look at the type of house – they're building them on the corner. Cheap rubbish – so that when the whites drive past they can say – "Oh, that's a shitting Coloured location", that's why they build them there. Why can't they build us decent places like everyone else has?'

The Need for a Revised Housing Policy
These feelings are prevalent and will have to be contended with if the Coloured person's bitterness is to be allayed. Part of the remedy is to realise the urgency for

good quality subsidised housing so that **everybody** in the Township will be given a date in the foreseeable future when they can live in decent conditions. There is also a need for home ownership to be introduced in the area so that people can invest in property and feel some security of tenure. A more realistic approach towards the Coloured people must become a priority. It must be made plain that the authorities are there to serve the community and understand their difficulties. The breakdown in communication is serious. Successful housing, community and rent schemes practised in other countries must be considered and introduced where possible.

Identity of the Coloured People

Yet over and above the demographic and socio-economic problems, I consider the **lack of identity** of the Coloured person to be the key issue around which revolves his personal despair. Primitive societies have always taken care over the socialisation of the young and been aware of the importance of relating the individual's position in a positive way to that of the society as a whole. Philosophers throughout the ages have taken as their starting point the question Who am I? A man needs a knowledge of himself, for what he is and how he perceives himself in relation to the people around him to a large extent determines how he will behave.

Regrettably, the effect of apartheid in South Africa has resulted in the Coloured people losing sight of their place and position in the total scheme of things: and this in turn is causing them to feel unwanted, divided amongst themselves, disillusioned and bitter. There is no clear official definition of a Coloured person.

Official Racial and Cultural Definition

Mann indicates that the: 'Definition of who is a Coloured and who is not is by no means easily achieved in practice;' (1957, p. 5) and that: 'The mixed-bloods of South Africa have been made by many races; they are not a race themselves and have no culture peculiarly their own; they are scattered in several discreet clusters.' (p. 8)

Van der Merwe notes that: 'In South African Law it has become customary to define the Coloured by **exclusion,**[7] ie a Coloured is a person who cannot be classified as White, Bantu or Asiatic.' (1957, p. 7) H. S. Coetzee makes the same point when he talks of the negative approach to Coloured people: *'die sê wat die Kleurling nie is nie . . . As hy nie iewers anders tuishoort nie, dan is hy 'n Kleurling.'* ('this describes what the Coloured is not . . . If he doesn't belong anywhere else, then he is a Coloured.') (1971, p. 31)

The Population Registration Act No. 30 of 1950 defines a Coloured person as one who in appearance is obviously not white and who is not a member of an aboriginal race or African tribe. Proclamation 46 of 1959 sub-divides Coloured people into seven groups: Cape Coloured, Malay, Griqua, Chinese, Indian,[8] Other Asiatic and Other Coloured. 'Other Coloureds' are those people who do not fall into any of these groups and who are not white or 'native' as defined in Section I of the Population Registration Act of 1950.[9]

In practice there are a number of conflicting administrative criteria, as one Coloured man in Western indicated. 'All right they've taken my house from me, I can't live where I want to, and now they want to rob me of the only other possession I have – my children, and they tell me they are not of my blood! . . . Can you explain it to me? I am a Cape Coloured – look here is proof, my identity card. My wife is a Cape Coloured, there see, there it's written; but our children are classified as "Other Coloured" – here in red writing on their identity cards – *Ander Gekleurde*. Now what's this Other Coloured business? Why are my children not classified like me and my wife, they're our blood . . . I'm going to Pretoria and I'll tell them what they can do about their bloody Other Coloured.' (His children were born in the Transvaal.)

Ethnologists thus far have not discovered a separate culture distinctive to Coloured people, so that generalisations about their cultural homogeneity even in the Cape need be accepted with caution: 'The Coloured people of the Cape Peninsula constitute a well-demarcated ethnic group with clearly recognisable features and characteristic cultural conditions. They have evolved over the course of three centuries out of the continuing intermingling of different racial strains, the most important being indigenous Hottentots and Bushmen, as well as Whites of different nations . . . and slaves who came largely from Madagascar or . . . India, Ceylon or Malaya . . . there has also been an element of Bantu racial stock.' (Gillis et al, 1973, p. 1374)

J. H. Coetzee emphasises that the term 'Coloured' is merely a generic term of external origin in the sense that it did not evolve out of a distinctive group. He shows how culturally, especially in their religion and value system, Coloured people model themselves on and have great affinity with the whites. But, he says: 'The great majority are border or "marginal" people. They veer away from the lowest ethnic level of black people but without total success. At the same time they passionately strive for acceptance by whites.'[10] (1971, p. 63)

Likewise the National Bureau of Educational and Social Research states: *'Op grond van taal, godsdiens en kultuur, kan die meeste Kleurlinge as behorende tot die Westerse kultuurgemeenskap beskou word.'* (NBOMN, 1964, pp. 71–72) ('On grounds of language, religion and culture, the majority of Coloureds can be regarded as belonging to the Western cultural community.') Cilliers also shows how Coloured people today are still a heterogeneous people with a variety of sub-groups. (1963, p. 23)

Implications of the Coloured Person's Marginality

A study by Mann helps us to understand the **implications** of the negative, uncertain and often conflicting definitions of what constitutes a Coloured person. He notes three psychological features characteristic of marginality, namely: 'insecurity feelings, self-pity and sensitivity' (1975, p. 139) though he believes these need not necessarily be related to race or nationality. However, such traits were repeatedly manifest in my interviews in Western Township. People would frequently despair of their plight but do little about it. Most of them found it difficult to mobilise into action when things went wrong, and they were always highly sensitive to comments made by others on matters which concerned them, above all on any situation that might suggest their inferiority.

Rifts within the Community

Adults in the Township would often say to me: 'The weakness of the Coloured people is that they are divided. They are too selfish. Look at the Bantu, the Whites, the Indians – if I have an old jersey from my child, when it's grown out of it I give it to my sister's children – but a Coloured, no, he won't do it.'

'The fault of the Coloureds, especially here in Johannesburg, is that they do not stand together, they are not united, each is only out for himself . . . Their biggest downfall is that they look at other Coloureds as '*laag*' ('low-down') . . . If you haven't got money they think you aren't worth talking to.'[11]

An Indian lady who had married a Coloured man was living in the flats in the Township. When they first got married they lived in one room with their children; it was very modest but they tried to keep it nice. She spoke of her Coloured in-laws: 'They were awful to me, and looked down on me . . . Now I have a nice flat and oh they come and talk and are glad to see me. I could say to them: "Why should I bother with you when you never helped me and looked down on me when I needed you" –

maar die Bybel sê dis nie reg om so te doen nie, en dit help niemand nie' ('but the Bible says it's not right to behave like that, it helps no-one.')

Adults describe the status-race in the redeveloped area: 'If your next door neighbour buys a good hi-fi then you must also buy such a good one, and if she gets a polisher then you must also get one or else you're looked down upon.'

A problem facing the community of which the inhabitants are acutely aware is that 'everyone tries to be white'. One lady defined this very clearly: 'Well there are three grades. At the top are those who look like Europeans: they are Grade I – the hair and complexion group. Grade II are on the sun-tan side, and Grade III are the dark group. Grade I looks on II as nothing even if they are educated, and I drinks heavily, but both I and II unite against III – they are nothing.'

My evidence largely supports this viewpoint. A fairly wealthy woman of the redeveloped area who could pass as white says: 'I have no trouble with apartheid. No, I have nothing to complain about there. I never go into a non-white post office, I always go into the white. And on the train I always travel in the white compartments, I won't just travel with every Dick, Tom and Harry.' She continued: 'I say the Kaffir who knows it's a Kaffir – he's all right. I've got a girl and she's O K, and she knows she's a Kaffir – she gives you no cheek, but it's this rubbish we're getting in Western. Look at it – half of Western is Black. I tell you – these aren't Coloured, this is a bloody Kaffir township. I want to clear out.'

She has given birth to all her children at a white Maternity Home. 'I know I pay more but I want the best treatment . . . I won't go to Coronation [the Coloured hospital]. I won't go to such a filthy Kaffir hospital. I said to my husband, you won't take me in there over my dead body. It stinks, there are cockroaches all over . . . I say that's a Kaffir hospital! When I'm sick I go to a European doctor . . . I've been going to him for eight years now and he knows me and we pay him . . . but that Coronation, there the bloody whites they just use us as their guinea-pigs. And I say I will be no guinea-pig for some white student to practise on. Why can't they practise on the whites?'

Other mothers bemoan the fact that the status race begins already at the birth of the child. 'When my baby was born, my relatives-in-law phoned the hospital and do you know what is the first thing they asked? *"Hoe lyk die baby? . . . Is hy baie donker? . . . het hy krul hare . . .?"* ' ('How does the baby look? . . . Is he very dark? . . . does he have curly hair . . . ?') She was so angry and sad that she replied: *'Hy lyk net soos sy pa'* ('He looks just like his father.')

When children are small there is the same problem: *'Die moeders sê vir hul kinders, hul moenie geselskap hou met dirty children.'* ('The mothers say to their children, they mustn't keep company with dirty children.') 'It's all the hair and complexion business. If you've got curly hair or dark skin the mothers say – don't play with the goldy-locks children, and if you're light the mothers say don't let me see you playing with those low-down children. Instead of everybody mixing because you're a person.'

Outside one house I used to see a little African boy of five who never talked or smiled but always lethargically played on his own with his hoop and stick. It transpired that his mother is African and is living with a Coloured man in the house. This was her child from a former marriage. They built on a room at the back of the man's mother's house. The African woman worked and always kept her room clean, simply furnished and homely. The entire Coloured family of the man's mother, sister, relatives and friends rejected the woman *'want sy is 'n native'* ('because she is a native') and when she and her man are at work during the day they continue to ostracise the little boy. They never talk to him, only shout at him and beat him. Now none of the children in the neighbourhood will play with him because he fights with them. His mother has stopped feeding him and buying him clothes.

In my last of many interviews the mother-in-law was beside herself with fury and grief because her son and the African woman had decided to marry. She forced them to send the child to the country as he wasn't Coloured, and booted them both out of the house for she wasn't going to have a 'Kaffir maid' as a daughter-in-law, although they had been happily living as man and woman for two years. They are now lodging with a woman who is an alcoholic and who needs their rent as income. The irate mother asserts that she agrees with Government legislation on this matter, saying that her son was causing a disturbance and that 'God is love and he will help me to live through these troubles, and in the end he is the judge.' There is great unease and tension.

At the same time and very quietly there are people who move out of Western and can pass and live as whites in white society just as there are those few Africans who also desire to upgrade themselves by passing into Coloured society. These desperate attempts for the 'better-life' and the double-life or total rejection of background they entail, cause great strain on all concerned. One woman who has passed for white regularly visits relatives in the Township and each time must park her car three blocks away so that no-one can recognise it. Her relatives can also never visit her at home. When they walk to the shops the woman keeps ducking under her jersey every time a car with a white person in it drives past lest it be one of her white friends who would then disown her. Other Coloured people regard those who act in this way as traitors to themselves.

On the one hand then it is true as Coloured people say, that 'the downfall of the Coloured is that he looks upon the next man as some other person – and not the same as him,' but on the other, it is vital that we recognise this attitude as a problem causing much confusion, rejection and lack of commitment.

The majority of inhabitants of Western Township are poor and struggling to live; they evince little in the form of self-help or healthy creative energy directed at fulfilling themselves as individuals or as a community – I believe, because they **feel nothing** for themselves in these roles.

When they do not respond to the few outlets there are such as sportsfields[12] and occasional meetings, I do not believe this is as some would say a conscious rejection of apartheid but rather a subconscious feeling of powerlessness, futility and indifference bred from hardship.

In his discussion of social malnutrition, Bell (1961, p. 131) stresses that a person has the 'need to feel needed and of value and importance to [the] group and society,' and that there is 'the need for a socially provided meaning and motivation for life and goals with clearly prescribed means of achieving those goals'. (p. 134) All these seem to be lacking in the Western community.

Repercussions of the Immorality Act

Very few of the people I spoke to were proud of being Coloured. On the contrary in almost all their actions they seek to emulate the 'superior' whites. Thus it seems necessary to think of the needs of the Coloured people not only in terms of socio-economics but with regard to their psychological disposition. In this respect it is my opinion that the Government must reconsider the Immorality Act,[13] primarily because the Coloured people in terms of this Act become unwanted and undesirable citizens of South Africa. My interpretation of the effect of this Act is that it serves to negate the Coloured person's sense of validity as a human being. His position becomes by implication that of a bastard, which lowers his sense of personal worth and causes an undercurrent of psychological discontent that lessens his commitment to the society at large.

The political and social definition of the Coloured people and where they belong in the South African ideology of Separatism must be clarified. Such a definition should in my opinion on no account embrace punitive legislation for those who have crossed the colour line. The pursuit of group identity is official policy, but we need to eradicate legislation that causes a miscarriage of life, which not only brings suffering to individuals but robs people of the will to exist and of pride in themselves. Such easing of legislation might marginally increase the number of inter-group marriages but it is more likely that most people for personal and social reasons will stay within their population groups. We also need to remember that much 'passing' from Coloured to White and African to Coloured is based on the increased economic and social privileges thereby attained. If all population groups in South Africa had equal rights and opportunities there would be little incentive to cross the colour-bar to adopt a false identity.

The Need for New Policies, Goals and Methods

It is important to remember that most Coloured people live in Western Township because they **have** to by official decision, and not because they want to. They feel a sense of alienation from all that goes on around them and confusion at being drawn into this problem-community. They know they are derided by others for living there. Most hate the Township or at best are fatalistically reconciled to it. They cannot find pleasure or security in their place of residence. Added to these burdens is the fact that they have been thrust with other people with whom they have little in common, despite being classified as Coloured.

Thus to give them a new, viable sense of identity, they must have assurances in real terms that they are desirable citizens whose present conditions and future expectations are a matter of concern to the country. The people need to be given goals and a feeling of being wanted. Many would agree with the man who said: 'We do not want to be white or have posh houses in the Northern suburbs, but we want to be **recognised as people** and get basic human rights . . . It is not so much a matter of colour but of dignity and opportunity . . . I don't mind living in Western so much, but I want freedom of movement and the same rights as the whites.'

In conclusion then, although political agitation appears to be minimal in the Township,[14] there is increasing impatience and bitterness over housing, high rents, and the attitudes of government authority, both white and Coloured. There are those who have been helped by the system, many who cherish acts of kindness by whites and help from the Government in education or maintenance, but the overriding atmosphere is rather one of restlessness, violence and tension. People have been patient, and it is salutary to know that there are still amenable people in Western, but for many their faith in the sincerity and goodwill of the authorities is beginning to crumble. As one lady said: 'The Government is always talking about terrorism, communism and things like that, but what do they give us? – nothing. O K. They have a mandate from the electorate for Bantustans, but do you know what's going to happen? The Kaffirs will get their independent states, but once you're independent and you see over there the gold mines, the diamond mines, the industry, and you've got nothing – I tell you, you'll go straight outside and take any means you can to get those for yourself.'

'They say the communists give us lies. Well I'll tell you something, we've had nothing but lies all our life. We've grown up on lies. We've had lies when we were small, lies when we grew up, lies when we're adults and I tell you, we're sick of their damn lies. So, they say the communists will give us lies – well I tell the Government that we're prepared to take those lies and see if they're different – maybe those lies will even bring us something.'

FOOTNOTES

1. Beinart (1965) observes: 'Western Native Township . . . existed from 1920 to 1962. Here the houses were small (400 sq. ft.) and facilities at the beginning were non-existent. But the [African] community worked hard at improving their environment. They fixed their houses, built fences, planted trees and organised themselves to keep their community healthy.

   To add space they enclosed the open porch of their houses and then decorated the 22′ × 7′ street-facing facade. The walls are painted with a few, bold elementary forms: circles, diamonds, stars, stripes, rectangles with indented round corners.' (pp. 20–21)
2. Facilities for the old area, which constitutes four-fifths of the Township, are as follows:

Facility lacking	*Est. %*	*Substitute*
No geyser	100%	(Stove)
No electric cooker	97%	(Coal Stove)
No bath	95%	(Tub/Basin)
No H. or C. tap inside	94%	(Cold Tap Outside)
No gas or electric lighting	91%	(Paraffin/Candles)
No heater	87%	(Cooking Stove)
No fridge	70%	(—)
No 2nd exit door	51%	(—)

3. A Johannesburg 'Sunday Times Extra' report on 15. 12. 1974 comments on similar problems in other areas: 'The Cape Town City Council has begun a full-scale investigation into allegations that certain officials entrusted with allocating dwellings in Coloured townships are favouring applicants who offer them presents of cash, appliances and sex.'
4. This figure is too low, but is important because it indicates what the people believe is the situation and their mistaken conception of aspects of white life. Nevertheless the conditions for whites are more favourable: the flats are sub-economic and the average white person earning R130 a month pays only R26 in rent.
5. Only three people are recorded as earning above this amount.
6. Since the average pension is R29,50 a month, it should be obvious that with electricity charges added this rate is too high.
7. My emphasis.
8. Indians are treated as a separate group in other legislation.
9. Statutes of South Africa, 1950, Proclamation 46, vol. 195, No. 6190 of the Population Registration Act, No. 30 of 1950.
10. Translated from the Afrikaans.
11. Adam Small has a similar comment to make on the Coloured politician: 'The image is one of self-destruction.' (*The Star,* 11. 11. 1974)
12. Which are not particularly inviting.
13. The Immorality Act of 1927 prohibited sexual intercourse between white and African. It was amended in 1950 (Immorality Amendment Act, No. 21) to extend to all blacks, which thus includes Coloured people. The Mixed Marriages Act, No. 55 of 1949, prohibits marriages between whites and blacks. (Statutes of South Africa)
14. Except for an alleged incursion of the Black Power movement encouraging gangsters to: 'go out and kill the whites, don't kill your own people'.

Chapter 9
Social Work and Community Rehabilitation

Western Township is thus an area of sub-standard housing characterised by neglect, overcrowding and their attendant social ills. It would be a challenge to the best social welfare department and a headache rather forgotten than tackled by others.

Social work is a particularly taxing vocation for work in an area such as this is tense and depressing. To see people without food in the house, children whose mothers have deserted them through marital difficulties, fathers breaking down because they cannot find the wherewithal to be fathers and get decent jobs, and families suffering acutely from overcrowding either makes one more compassionate and efficient or more hardened and remote. The social worker's reaction to the situation is an important part of the therapy of an area.

I should like to make a series of suggestions to social workers and welfare departments for I believe that in a deprived community such as Western they should act as a major catalyst for change. If I am critical it is not to decry the good work done and help already given to people in need, but rather because I believe social welfare is at present too limited and its programmes insufficiently community centred. There is dire need in Western Township for social workers to effect an energetic and imaginative programme for the upliftment of the community as a whole and the individual as a part of it.

As indicated in previous chapters, the very poor of the Township do not talk politics: they are too depressed and too feverishly trying to make ends meet or too apathetic and cowed down by life. But the culture of poverty is disturbing and unstable, especially where relationships are so tenuous that the value of human life has little meaning any longer – a danger sign for any society.

Financial hardship is a genuine consideration in evaluating the quality of life in a society. In consequence of it, essential foods, medical treatment and cultural necessities are often unavailable. Not only are families in Western adversely affected by poor wages, or good wages but high rent, but the pensioners also find life very hard.

It is pitiful to meet people who are ageing living in an invidiously dependent situation: in many houses the old granny sleeps on the concrete floor whilst the other adults are in a bed, though they do at least tolerate her. Many pensioners are invaluable assets to the working family and instrumental in socialising the children and providing them with stability, especially when their mother drinks; but too many are tired and suffering from ill-health and should have greater choice of the way they would like to spend their old age. In this respect the new two-roomed houses built for pensioners in the Township are not a viable alternative, for the rents and electricity leave them with a mere R10,50 a month to live on.[1] Some are quite enterprising and sell *vetkoekies* (fat cakes) or *koeksisters* (plaited strips of pastry, fried then dipped in syrup) or sweets to children; still others sell meat or fruit or do washing; but others would rather rest a little, be relieved of their responsibilities or undertake less arduous activities. There is a need to develop the role of the pensioner in the community, to provide more facilities for the aged, and to see that they are adequately housed for a nominal rent.

I have demonstrated how people are tending to overspend in the Township and are thus weighed down by hire-purchase debts. One of my informants who at 45 receives a widow's pension of R32 a month, bought a luxurious new lounge suite for R400 for which she must pay R20 a month in hire-purchase. She is still paying off R8 a month for her R200 coal stove.

There is no question that every family has the right to enjoy the material comforts that make life more pleasurable. One needs however to instil a sense of proportion in relation to means. Budgeting books[2] which inculcate realistic yet flexible spending patterns would be of assistance; other aspects are more difficult to implement. Laws are needed to curb advertising which lures people to excessive spending for status reasons; legislation is required to prevent exploitation of the poor by excessively high hire-purchase commitments. But the two most intangible yet powerful factors causing the Coloured person in Western Township to overspend are his economic and political situation.

People everywhere tend to be haphazard in their use of money, but **it is precisely the deprived person who will need to buy unnecessary goods to compensate for his psychologically deprived condition and lack of fulfilment in other roles.** A man's perception of himself in relation to the society at large influences his value system. The Coloured people of Western Township are attempting to become acceptable as people by acquiring the outward symbols of white success – ie possessions. Coloured men in particular are aware that equal pay for equal work and a free labour market are not yet implemented; that they lack a real function in South African society at large, in Western Township as a community, and in their own families in cases where they may be economically dispensable. Men in particular are grossly overspending on drink, a symptom of their lack of purpose.

Thus I have urged that the political structure as a whole must give the Coloured people a positive sense of identity and a sense of worth. This is the root malady of many of their problems.

A Rational Approach to Abortion

An investigation into the rôle of the Coloured man in Western is important, for his confusion at his inability to support a family and his feelings of being superfluous tend to lead to a discarding of his responsibility towards his children and wife, and a loss of affinity towards his fellows.

In this respect the burden also weighs heavily on the woman who must often bear a double load in rearing her children, and in turn the children, who are not properly cared for, in their anguish stab the society that gave them birth. The question of contraception needs to be handled more realistically and with greater understanding. We also need to re-examine objectively the ethics of abortion. In the first place preventive contraception should be our ideal for planned parenthood. But if it fails, abortions conducted in a medically sound environment are infinitely more desirable than those undertaken by crude methods under the dubious circumstances of a slum toilet. Furthermore, it is surely unethical for society to forbid a woman the individual right to terminate the birth of her child when she feels she cannot cope with it psychologically or financially, and when she is not provided with adequate alternatives by that same society.

In 1966 Forssman and Thuwe conducted a study of children born in Sweden to mothers who had been refused legal abortion. All except one of the children were detrimentally affected in their mental health, social adjustment and educational level. The unwanted children were part of a syndrome of instability at home, did not enjoy a secure childhood and fewer were reared by their own parents than the control children. 'They were also registered more often in psychiatric services . . . more often . . . for antisocial and criminal behaviour, and slightly more often for drunken misconduct . . . More of them were educationally subnormal and far fewer had pursued . . . studies over and above what is obligatory . . . The differences between the two series . . . were often statistically significant, and when they were not significant they always pointed in the same direction – to the unwanted children being born into a worse situation than the control children.' (p. 87)

The quality of life a society can offer the newly-born child, and the ability of the authorities to provide the child with satisfactory housing and adequate schooling at all levels, plus sufficient food and care, medical aid, and recreational outlets, are surely a more valid criterion than forcing the existence of the child into a world which by its lack of provision shows it does not really want it.

Finally, our present laws and thinking on the question of legitimacy and the position of the man and woman involved require re-thinking. It is unsound that the woman or the state (via maintenance grants) should be held solely responsible for the birth of the child, for this is tending to breed irresponsibility and a sense of ineffectuality in the Coloured male. We need to define the man's social and legal role more clearly so that he will be encouraged to be involved with, and attached to his child. He must either be held responsible for the child he fathers or take greater care that contraceptive precautions are practised.

The Seriousness of the Housing Situation

I have mentioned the seriousness of the housing situation in Western Township; the frustrations and bitternesses and the growing impatience of the inhabitants at the Housing Division's seeming imperviousness to their pleas for new dwellings; that four-fifths of the people are living in unsatisfactory two to three-roomed houses and that families are growing up in overcrowded, inadequate dwellings. The people are also upset at the blanket criteria used in allocating housing: 'We are not graded according to our ability . . . we have no choice in choosing the type of dwelling we want to go to.' They resent the perpetual arguments: 'The council says you don't have a house for your things, only a roof over your head. But I say, a fridge and a kitchen unit are a **necessity.** You can't go out at night here. It's too dangerous. Home is our place. A person can't just go to work and sleep and work all his life – he must have something to do . . . ag, living here people go down.'

The system of housing people in the Township needs to be carefully considered so that families can work towards home ownership. At the same time rentals and wages need to be constantly adapted to meet the exigencies of living. Alternative housing with modern conveniences must be provided in the immediate future with State subsidies on high rentals.

The presence of vandalism and the perpetual disposal of rubbish over household fences into the road are further symptoms of psychological malaise.[3]

The Role of the Social Worker

Most urgent steps are thus necessary to improve the lot of the Coloured inhabitants of Western on a Governmental and local level.

In view of the circumstances the first essential for an effective social welfare department must be to have at least one social worker who at any given time, walks the streets of such a Township, does house visiting and through establishing friendly contacts with people, is able to draw a realistic human sketch of the problems of the area, with possible recommendations for treatment.

By this method, it should be possible to locate the families who need help but do not know how to get it. When I visited Mrs Hansen she was working in her kitchen doubled-up with severe backache and cooking the last potatoes in the house. She was not self-pitying but said that though she and her husband had been happily married he had now gone insane. She cannot get maintenance for her 10 children because he is not completely insane and for this reason the Kimberley doctor who first attended to him would not send him to Sterkfontein.[4]

Although welfare departments need certain bureaucratic guidelines and adequate documentation of cases, their weakness is that they tend to become bogged down in over-documentation. In a genuine situation such as that of Mrs Hansen a special case should be made of which only the main points need be noted. Flexibility is a crucial element in a lively system.

On the other hand, face-to-face contact with the community enables a worker to administer to people who simply need some friendly 'supervision'. A case in point is Francis who, out of R80 a month she receives as maintenance for her daughter's illegitimate children, is paying out R40 on hire-purchase for a hi-fi. Both she and Mrs Hansen need kindly practical guidance.

It would be an excellent service to the community if the Welfare Department were to establish a cheerful stimulating office **in Western Township** to which people could come for help. It was most distressing to hear remarks like: 'No I won't go for help to the social worker. She just shouts at us and is not interested to help,' or: 'That social worker keeps you waiting half a morning and then she moans at you. She won't help me.' The people repeatedly found the social workers connected with the Township harsh and lacking in understanding. Although one can empathise with the feelings of despair and weariness of social workers, community responses are necessary indices of the success of a service.

Although social workers have to face practical situations and mobilise people out of the inertia of existence, it is disturbing that their training inadequately enables them to come to grips with the **root causes** of individual problems. They were frequently accused of moralising at their clients. 'Well if he wouldn't spend so much money on drink, then he would have food!' It is quite untherapeutic that professional social workers tell people they are useless when what so many are needing is just a sense of worth and purpose and a little understanding and incentive. And it is wrong that I should phone the Johannesburg Coloured Social Welfare Department to inform them that three women are sleeping in devastating conditions out in the veld in Western in cold wet weather, and be told: 'If they need help so badly they can walk, can't they?'

There are two major weaknesses in social work as it is practised in Western Township. The first is that a white middle-class concept is being applied to a group of people who do not necessarily share the same values even when the administrators are Coloured. Thus, instead of going into the Township to find out what the **people** want, social workers give them what they think they should have. Accordingly, Mr Venter (see pp. 52–54) receives R35 a month maintenance (on which one supposes he can support seven children) but nothing is done about his basic problem – the will to live.

The second weakness is the case-method. When one asks social workers why they rebuke their clients so much, they will say: 'There are just too many people to see. I get overworked and irritable and I just get furious at the way they live.' There is no doubt that case-studies are valuable and necessary tools to be used in certain complex instances – though a sensitive comprehensive study need not take longer than two hours. It is however my opinion that social workers are taking too much time documenting individual case-studies with the result that they cannot cope with the problems of the whole community.

The Need for a New Approach

There is something badly wrong in Western when many mothers tell me either that they can't rear their children there or that they need to find an Institution for them.

I should like to see the Departments of Social Welfare and social workers such as those serving Western Township viewing the individual as a microcosm of society as a whole. The problems of Western are also the by-product of various features of our society and the Department of Social Welfare must generate improvements in every sphere where it is aware the individuals of such a Township are deprived. This could take many forms.

First it calls for some reorganisation within the Department. I would suggest that departments periodically employ an effective team of consultants to help them improve their running efficiency and the quality of service provided. This would ensure that new ideas and methods are injected into what can otherwise become a very tired machine. Many firms and universities are constantly evaluating – what are we aiming at, how do we get there, how are we functioning, how could we improve? There are always people in large departments who are less sensitive than others, less skilled, and who block help to families in need. A team of experts could help devise an in-built system to help counter such blocks and give the clients channels of appeal or room for making suggestions. People need to feel they can go to a Department of Social Welfare to get advice or help in a friendly and practical way; and if they are too confused or troubled or neglectful to go there, then the Department must go to them. It is wasteful to poor people to undertake needless repetitive visits, as one person said: *'ah dis so lastig jy moet so baie keer na hulle gaan, en dan weet jy nie of hulle jou sal help.'* ('oh, it's so tiresome, you have to go in so often, and then you still don't know whether they will help you.') For many of the people in need in Western, 20 cents for transport on each visit to the Department is too much money to spend.

Once social workers feel the pulse of the community they can create opportunities for the upliftment, self-help, and channelising of the creative energies of the people. For instance, at present there is only one crèche in the entire Township. In such a case the Social Welfare Department should indicate the need for more crèches to the Central Government. But at the same time it could initiate a Play Centre on one of the football fields and bring in mothers and even gangsters to re-direct peoples' energies into a useful and fulfilling programme of activity. Play groups run by mothers would cost the Department very little, but once initiated and with quarterly meetings for new ideas, could lead to more emotionally and intellectually aware children being prepared for school.

Weekly in Western, mothers will tell you of a child knocked over or run down by a car. Heavy vehicles stampede down the tarred roads where the children play.[5] Here again, social workers could demand that speed restrictions be introduced and enforced in the Township and ask teachers and volunteers or the Traffic Department to institute a Road Safety Programme.

This type of sensitive awareness to what is bothering them is what the people are missing in Western, and why they so often say: 'nobody cares.'

The Use of Volunteers

I feel that social workers are making a mistake by not utilising the resources available from volunteers and local inhabitants. People in Western need to be drawn out of themselves and into the community – they need to become creatively involved in other people. One of the best ways of achieving this must surely be to encourage a person who has a talent to teach it to others. There could be demonstrations of cooking, home decorating and repairs, budgeting and saving, home nursing, basic carpentry and plumbing, do-it-yourself, car maintenance, sewing and mending, book and record clubs, handicrafts, educational films, drama groups, typing courses, topical lectures and discussions and a local newspaper, with responsibility for each activity being lodged in a group of interested or gifted people. Organised communication of groups which fail, and feedback from those which succeed are all part of the process.

The possibilities are endless at all levels of the community and need only involve the social worker or Community Planner at intervals, but the people at the top must **believe in** the inhabitants, and the volunteers or staff, and in the need for a creative community life. A start must be made at diverting and uplifting these people from their fears, obsessions and depressions.

I am aware that Governmental Departments have tight budgets but is not money better spent on preventive rather than punitive measures? From the financial angle as well effective use of volunteers is a cost-saving measure quite apart from its highly beneficial effect on community involvement.

I would not only recommend volunteer work from the people of Western Township themselves but would suggest that young people from outside the Township work in such an area, becoming involved in activities which demand enthusiasm and energy rather than trained skills. Girls during the year that boys do their military service could have the option of serving their society voluntarily in the field of social welfare by becoming active in crèches, library readings, old-age homes, helping TB patients or similar activities in the poorer areas of all population groups.

It is imperative that work such as that of SANCA be extended and allied more closely to the community and that by poster campaigns and other methods, the fears of treatment and other negative reactions of the inhabitants are met.

It is vital that the Department should tackle the **causes** of gangsterism and initiate youth programmes. A team of psychiatrists and social workers (not policemen) should also be made available to handle the gangs in the Township by providing them with constructive work and a sense of purpose in life so that people will find it safe to visit and relax in a freer way by day and night; work must also be done at a community and familial level to integrate the male into the community in a meaningful way; and to provide counselling for individuals with problems, eg acute feelings of failure.

Marriage Guidance and Child Welfare societies should be given entrance into the community.

The Department responsible for Coloured education must see to the quality and quantity of schooling provided. Preventive dentistry and medicine should be available, especially for all pre-school children.

Coloured people need to have access to live theatre or symphony or jazz concerts, preferably in white areas, but otherwise in their own.

The present planning and administration of housing in Western Township need be completely overhauled; and redevelopment of the Township must be considered as a matter of urgency.

Sufficient subsidised holiday areas should be established to allow poor Coloured people to have a holiday outside townships such as Western and thus experience a change of environment and thinking.

A national wage at the minimum effective level need be enforced by law according to rural and urban costs of living. Coloured men and women should be able to find fulfilment in work by being paid the rate for the job and through a steady relaxation of job reservation be rewarded by promotion for good work.

Legislation should be passed making it an offence for a person to be abused at work on the basis of his racial classification and employers should develop means of coping with this circumstance.[6]

Coloured people should receive full recognition of their needs in Parliament and a clear sense of identity.

The Coloured Representative Council could actively identify itself with the Township and its problems.

Things must begin to happen in Western, so that the inhabitants can sense that other people, and the country as a whole, care about their wellbeing. This kind of organisation can be multiplied and extended at all levels.

I feel that a Department of Social Welfare has a right, and duty, to advise other departments such as housing – where their activities are not sufficiently promoting the interests of a particular community. Where factories are paying women a wage of only R10 a week and families are simply not making ends meet, then a Labour Department Official should be contacted to rectify the situation.

The People must be Involved in Decision-Making

Finally, in all planning affecting Coloured people of Western Township, it is essential that they themselves are incorporated both in the decision-making, the implementation and the evaluation of the programme. **Only when people begin to have some say in how they live do they become interested in the quality of their environment.** The way of life of Western Township is illustrative of a people who have had no choice as to where or how they should live, whose opinion is never asked for and whose feelings are of no concern to the planners. This is acutely detrimental both psychologically and socially.

Furthermore it is possible that unless immediate action is taken to diffuse the tension within the Township, in the not too distant future we may find the bitter frustrations and hatred exploding beyond its boundaries. Naturally families with a variety of problems will always be a part of human society and will need special care, for which I hope social workers will increasingly be trained in the the use of psychiatric methods.

Yet a slum such as Western demands a highly-faceted, energetic and organised programme. It is my hope that this will materialise so that the children of tomorrow need not suffer like the children of today.

FOOTNOTES

1. Pension = R29,50; Rent = R11; Electricity = R8 (per month).
2. A leading bank provides excellent books for the people of the wealthier northern suburbs of Johannesburg to assist them in developing sound spending habits.
3. The Johannesburg Municipality sends at least four trucks and men with shovels to clear the rubbish weekly, over and above the normal refuse removal.
4. A mental hospital. There are insufficient facilities for the mentally disturbed and handicapped.
5. Only main roads are tarred: subsidiary roads are untarred and in poor condition.
6. The Bantu Administration Act of 1927 [Section 29 (1)] prohibited the fomenting of hostility between African and white people. In 1974 this was extended to all race groups under Section I of the Second General Law Amendment Act, No. 94. (Statutes of South Africa)

Three Case Studies

1. The Bradshaws: Where God Provides

Mr and Mrs Bradshaw are pensioners and with them in their two-roomed house live their 28 year old mentally defective son, their 32 year old son who is married and has five children but who at present is alone and out of work; Margaret van Zyl, their married daughter, and her two children, and two grandchildren who attend school in the Township since the school in their home at Eldorado Park is not yet complete. (Their father usually brings R5 a week for their food.)

As I enter the house, the eldest brother is wiping the breakfast crumbs off the table: half a loaf of white bread and black tea. Margaret is soaking her feet in a bowl of hot water and is still in her nylon nightie. She looks young and frail. Sitting on the couch are granny and grandpa Bradshaw, playing with Margaret's baby.

The Bradshaw's daughter

Margaret, their daughter, is a bit depressed: she is on sick leave and has no money, but she agrees with her mother that she must go and work for money for her children, especially now that her husband is also ill. Margaret was hit on the head in the street in March last year and since then has suffered a nervous breakdown. She has had one once before. She is being treated by the psychiatrist at the Johannesburg General Hospital who treated her previously. The family can't raise 40 cents for her bus fare but believe that 'by tomorrow the Lord will provide'.

Her husband

Margaret is small, delicate and pretty, but her eyes are sunken with tiredness. Her mother says she suffers from piles and asks if I know a remedy for her. Margaret is 23 but has known her husband since she was 10. They got married at 17 and after two years had their first child. But the marriage is about to break down. Her husband is 31: he too was knocked down by someone in the street and hit on the head. He is now ill and has had to leave his job, so they have no income. He has gone to live with his mother in another part of Western, but the mother-in-law is dreadful to Margaret so she never goes there. 'Anyway he used to drink so much that most of his money got frittered away on alcohol.' She doesn't drink or smoke. Although she and her husband talk they no longer get on together, and she has been to the Marriage Guidance people to ask for a divorce. 'They say she'll probably get it, because he came and took his clothes away from there.'

One Saturday the whole relationship climaxed. Her husband came to their house and smashed the furniture. She took me over to see it. It was like a shattered building with broken bits and pieces left where they had fallen. He had broken the doors on their two wardrobes, ripped off the covers of the kitchenette drawers, and broken other chairs and a table. The little five year old daughter systematically pointed to all the damage. His intention had clearly been to destroy what had meant so much to them, and was a sad tribute to frustrated human anger.

Margaret never wants to see her married home again and feels sickened by what her husband has done. Her family is worried that if he does this to the furniture, he will next do it to her. Margaret says her five year old daughter becomes very angry about it all but is afraid of her father, especially as he is so big, and says she doesn't want to see him again. She doesn't think the child is disturbed by the events because she calls her grandfather 'father'.

Mr and Mrs Bradshaw

Mr Bradshaw at 65 is merry, wrinkled and kindly. A friend of his once asked the little granddaughter what she would do when Mr Bradshaw died. She said she would go in the grave and die with him. He is unfailingly affectionate to her and the other children: a thoroughly likeable and sensible man.

Mr Bradshaw has been down to the rent office and explained Margaret's position. They say that as long as she continues to pay the rent of R6 a month she can stay in the house, even though it's in her husband's name.

Mr and Mrs Bradshaw are two very lovable people. They are good-natured, easy-going and peaceful, propelled by an intense religious faith. There is none of the rasping talk between them and their children that one hears in other households.

Both the Bradshaws get R26 a month pension. On asking them about it, Mrs Bradshaw said: 'When I get my R26 a month pension, to me it is like a million pounds! And I go and pay my R6 rent and then my heart is at rest and we can buy the things we need. I am thankful for that money for we do not work for it.' They have meat about once a week, but vegetables and fresh milk they do without because these are too dear. As long as Mrs Bradshaw can make some porridge in the pot for the children, they are satisfied.

Mr Bradshaw's faith

Mr Bradshaw is a war veteran and proudly tells me of his war experiences. He fought in the Battle of Alamein and saw the entire 5th Brigade wiped out except for one man who now works at a shop in Johannesburg. Mr Bradshaw used to drink and gamble a lot and then suddenly during the war: 'God spoke to me and saved me.' He became an Apostolic and has lived and been powered by his faith ever since. He sums up the war by saying: 'We had hard times but we also had good times.' He remembers vividly how: 'I shook the hand of Haile Selassie!'

His language is constantly punctuated with religious quotations and beliefs. He has religious sayings and pictures all about the house. His most delightful one is a hanging over the doorway leading into the bedroom; he explains that if a smoker comes into his house, he takes this plaque and turns it back to front, so that it reads:

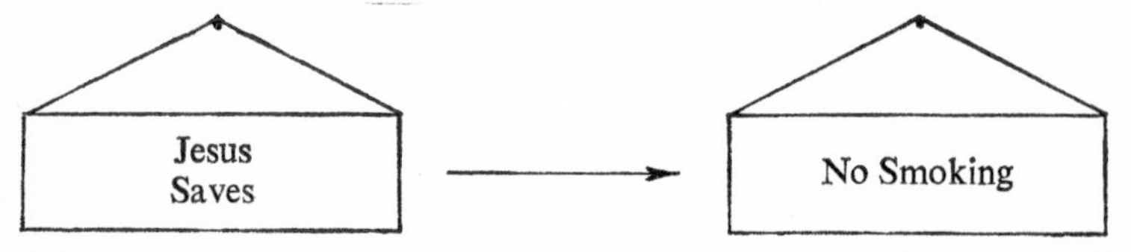

Mr Bradshaw and his family are satisfied with their very modest house for: 'If God has given you a table, you mustn't go and make the street your table.' And he will often tell you that God said: 'I am the Way, the Truth and the Life,' and this is the life one must follow. If anyone says he can't do something he says: ' "can't" is the name I give to the devil' and this motto has sustained them throughout their married life.

Mr Bradshaw used to be a heavy duty driver for a large cooldrink firm, but on medical advice he was pensioned off because it was making him ill. There are many proofs he draws upon to show how God has blessed his life.

One day he was driving the cooldrink truck to town and God whispered in his ear, so he took his foot off the accelerator. The African man next to him said: *'Oupa, wat doen jy?'* ('Grandpa, what are you doing?') He said he did not know but God had sent him a message that something was going to happen.

A police car was driving in front of him and the robot turned red. Mr Bradshaw put his foot on the brakes but they failed. He pulled the handbrake and slightly bumped the police car. The policeman got out and said: 'Just what do you think you are doing?'

Mr Bradshaw will talk at great length of how he used to think he had luck when gambling but 'only now since God is my helper do I have real luck'. He also believes that: 'Each time you have a drink, you add a wrinkle to your face.'

He takes a lively interest in the children and sits contented and jolly in his meagre surroundings. He shows me his well-thumbed Bible: 'So worn that I can't even take it to Church any longer.' He and his wife say that through their religion they 'don't drink, smoke or do anything wrong'. They feel their Church gives them something to go by. They have been married many years now 'not like these young people today'.

Mrs Bradshaw's resilience

Mrs Bradshaw has a patient, understanding face with loving eyes: one feels she has suffered and borne a lot, but has inner strength. She says they are not supposed to help their children with their pension, 'but what can you do if they need help?' She knows her direction in life, is clear in her decisions and gives her children advice, but feels that: 'Margaret must make up her own mind what she wants to do with her husband.' Her eldest son used to drink a lot but she told him that if he wanted to stay in her house then he was not to drink.

She never had a mother and was brought up by another woman, but has had to work most of her life. She has suffered a lot 'but God has always provided'. She never grumbles about having very little because she says: 'We must just take each day as it comes, and God will give us sufficient for that day.' She is pleased to help her daughter because 'what would Margaret do if she had all these troubles and her mother was dead?'

One gains the impression that Mrs Bradshaw goes through life clear-headed and with human understanding, aware of the futility of self-pity. She suffers from high blood-pressure so has someone in to do the washing once a week. Both she and her husband pay R1,90 a month in burial fees, seemingly unendingly, 'otherwise you could not be buried'.

One leaves such people with an uplifted spirit for they have found a way to cope with life though they know its harshness. When I left they asked me not to forget them, and the lady with the grey hair said they would be praying for me, my husband, and my home!

2. Piet: A Picture of the Gangs

Piet is a lively boy whose father died of a rheumatic heart disease when he was two. He and his mother live in a simple, friendly home. They have a lodger, a quiet man of 40 who is on a disability grant. This man was stabbed by gangsters in the pelvis some years ago and this has affected the movement in his legs.

Piet is a wiry, energetic eight year old who always told me much about the gangs before he hopped off to school. He would pop up with: *'My cousin was in die tronk gewees. Hy is net nou terug. Hy het iemand gemoor en 'n kar gesteel – in die dorp in. Hy was in die tronk vir twee jaar gewees.'* ('My cousin was in jail. He is now back. He murdered someone and stole a car in the town. He was in prison for two years.') He offered this as a sprightly bit of information to which no positive or negative morality was attached. Mary, his mother, was more reticent about it: *'Ah die kinders – hul vertel als.'* ('Oh the children – they tell all.')

The cousin is boarding with Mary now. He is working again but in the evenings and at weekends he sniffs Bostik and dagga – *'dit maak hom mal'*. ('This makes him mad.') When I asked if the cousin was in a gang, Piet replied merrily: *'Nee, hy is sy eie gang!'* ('No, he's his own gang!') But he says his cousin is often cruel to him and Piet has an awesome fear of him. The cousin takes Piet's ear and tweaks it hard, or pushes his head on the floor and stamps on it for no apparent reason, especially when he's 'high'. Mary acquiesces: *'Hy is rof met hom. Ek hou ook nie daarvan nie wanneer hy so met Piet doen.'* ('He is rough with him. I also don't like it when he does that to Piet.')

The cousin was at Leeukop Prison for hard labour. There he would receive *'harde pap en gravy, tee, amper nooit vleis en partykeer groente'* ('hard porridge and gravy, tea, seldom meat and sometimes vegetables.')

Gang life as seen through Piet's eyes

Piet would rattle off all the gangs to me. The dominant ones to his mind were the 'Riders', 'Big Guns', and 'Little Guns'. He says the gang members don't molest the little children unless they see them going to the shops with money. Then they will take the money from them.

He explains how the gang members buy and smoke dagga. *'Hulle breek die nek van die bottel af en sit die dagga daarin en dan suig hulle dit.'* ('They break the neck of the bottle and put the dagga in it and then they suck it.') They also smoke it with water. Other gangs draw benzine. They take the top off the bottle, put a cloth over it and inhale through the mouth. Piet's two equally chirpy friends arrived and confirmed this and also the fact of inhaling Bostik. They have seen the gangsters squeeze Bostik tubes and suck them. *'Dit droog op die longe en hulle word mal.'* ('It dries up the lungs and they go mad.') Sometimes when they're sniffing Bostik they spit the stuff on the walls as they pass.

Piet launched into various things he'd seen the gang members do. Once a lady was getting off the train at the station and one of them tripped her and they snatched her bag and ran away. Others just go about at night and stab any person they see. 'One man ran away but was stabbed in the face. They do that even if they don't know him.'

When the gangs fight they use pangas, knives, wires, stones and glass. Suddenly they chase a member of another gang and break flowers, fences and everything while they run *'en hulle kan so flits oor die fense spring'* ('and they can scale a fence like lightning.') When a gang war is in progress they sometimes hurl stones at windows or anything they see. They try to hurt each other, even kill. They will get hold of a chap and stab him *'totdat hy in die hospitaal moet lê. Daardie ander outjie hulle het hom op sy gesig geskeer en op sy rug'* ('until he has to lie in hospital. That other chap they scarred him on the face and on his back with a razor.') Sometimes after they've been fighting they call a truce; then they signal 'V' – a victory sign using two fingers.

Another little boy would join us and Piet would say quite unabashedly: *'Sy broertjie is deur die Riders dood gemaak.'* ('His little brother was killed by the Riders.') Another boy's cousin was stabbed across the back but survived. Another boy's father came home from a party after having had drinks and was stabbed and killed by *tsotsis*.

They twice repeated the story of a young woman who was attacked in the strip of grass at the end of the road with her baby on her back. The gangsters hacked both her and her baby up into little bits. *'Die mense het hulle daar net begrawe.'* ('The people buried them just there.') Another man was attacked in that area and a woman called the police: *'Die volgende dag het die mortuarily van hom kom haal.'* ('The next day the mortuarily [mortuary] van came to fetch him.')

One incident which amazed them was when they were at the shops. An African lady was buying her groceries and had put her large handbag between her legs on the ground. Suddenly *''n jongetjie stoot haar, neem die bag en hardloop weg'* ('a boy pushed her, took the bag and ran away.') Then the gang members gave chase and caught the boy and brought the bag back to the lady. She then opened her purse and gave each member R1. (This is a handsome reward.) This they found most strange.

Piet's leisure activities

Much of his free time is spent playing dice 'with 5 cents and proper gambling dice' and football on the machine in the café, though the older boys often bully them and take their money. He goes to the films, especially to see 'cowboys and crooks' and 'love-scenes', but not to Newclare because 'the cinema has bugs'. His favourite is going to the community hall where a man teaches them to box: 'boxing en Karate chop.' This he pays 5 cents a week for, and the activity appears to be run nightly, except for Sunday, at a nominal fee. He and his friends also play skittles with tins, hopscotch, and a variety of improvised can and ball-games.

In all his actions Piet displays creativity and imagination. He and his friends were always very curious. On one occasion they asked what my tape-recorder was and wanted to hear their voices. It was impossible to get them to stand away from the microphone because they were imitating the jazz singers who hold the microphone at the mouth and swing the chord to and fro in the other hand. All their songs were the rock-love songs of western societies. 'Oh won't you take me to the Mardi Gras'; 'Oh baby-hu-hu.' The recording was hopeless, the experience hilarious. They spent half the time deciding what they would say and the other half saying the machine wasn't working because they couldn't hear the immediate sound of their voice as you do on stage. Then when I would play their songs back to them they'd join in the singing and not hear themselves! With a magnanimous gesture Piet and Jody announced that the other kids must have a turn. But they were relatively dull and waited so long that they hadn't a chance and were swamped again by another deluge of stories.

After such a visit I was usually delighted and exhausted. So many children would have poured in and related their colourful fantasies. The cantankerous granny next door would call her children to work, but Mary would quietly join in or listen to the babble graciously.

School becomes dull

Piet and his friends attend the local school. They don't like it particularly and say the teachers shout 'all the time' and become cross quickly and cane even for little things or 'if you don't do your homework'. But they don't find school very interesting. In contrast with the excitements of life they have discovered, perhaps that isn't very surprising.

3. Betty: Patience and Understanding

Betty Snyman looks quite well, is plump and in her fifties, speaks quite good English and fluent Coloured-style Afrikaans. She wears a tattered dress, saying: 'It's better to wear dark clothes, they don't show the dirt.'

Her sons

Betty has five children, the eldest of whom lives in Bosmont and is married. 'He is a silk-screener and a good lad.'

The second eldest son is in Leeukop prison, north of Johannesburg, serving a 12 year prison sentence. He murdered a man together with two other men. She can visit him every first Sunday of the month but hasn't been very often lately. She visited him at Christmas. He is in good health but from his eyes she can see that he isn't happy and 'he isn't really all right. He said: "Every day in prison is two days less of your life . . . " but it's too late for him now.'

The other two young men, the co-murderers, have been let free. She has heard that even though one of them actually stabbed the victim, they had money and paid an attorney who got them off without sentence. But even if she hadn't been poor, Betty wouldn't have fetched an attorney 'because that man they killed might also have a wife and children and relatives who are crying tears because he is dead. My son must learn that you can't do things like that.'

Hendrik to be convicted for rape

Her fourth eldest is a boy of 14. He had been convicted for rape at the time of my first visit and was in a 'Home of Safety' whilst undergoing trial. She was going to go to the 'Council' before this happened to get him removed from the Township. She says she doesn't want to go to prison on account of her children. She was due to go to Court to hear when sentence would be passed.

This son, Hendrik, got into one of the Township gangs and together with two other boys raped a Black girl of 19. Betty thinks they will give him a sentence of six months, but she would 'prefer him to have a much longer sentence and be sent to one of the prisons in the Cape, away from here, where he can come out and have learnt a trade and got some discipline. He needs that. Otherwise he will just return and loaf about the street and get into trouble again.'

'That Bantu girl he raped had been fetched by the Coloured family from the farm to be their domestic servant. She's a strapping girl.' Betty fears repercussions from the Black people because of this.

Both these sons left school in Standard 6 and 5 by default. The one who raped kept saying he was going to school, but one day his mother followed him and saw him going into the fields to meet the gang. Then she went to his school and the teacher said he was just about to write a letter to her as her son had been absent from school so often. She had always found it strange when she asked about his homework; he said they never had any.

Betty feels that the local teachers do not set as much of an example as they should to the children. 'The one my son had used to drink heavily and send the children to the bottle store to fetch booze for him during schooltime.'

Hendrik and gang life

I went to see Betty to find out her son's rape verdict. She welcomed me in, even though 'I am still not straight yet'. I sat in her little verandah addition as the house was crowded.

I tentatively asked how Hendrik's case had gone and to my surprise she hushedly pointed out that he was there in the kitchen ironing his shirt. I remarked on how young and strong he looked. Betty whispered that he was still in one of the gangs and his case was still pending. I remarked how good it was he could iron his own shirt: he smiled and said nothing. Betty said, yes, she makes them wash and iron their own clothes 'or else they do nothing'. He had slept in a white overall, the type that Black cleaners wear in the city, and now was preparing his clothes for the day. He left the house at 10h00, the time the gang members usually begin to emerge into the street.

Betty said she didn't know what his sentence would be because he had 'gone and done' another misdeed: this would worsen his sentence. *'Ek hoor dat hy en sy vriende het 'n gang fight gehad en hulle het iemand van daardie ander gang seer gemaak, en die seun wat seer gekry het, lê daar buite die huis. Toe hulle veg is Hendrik en 'n ander gang mens in die huis gesluit: en toe was hulle gevang.'* ('I hear that he and his friends had a gang fight and they hurt one of that other gang, and the boy who was hurt lay outside the house. When they fought, Hendrik and another gang member were locked in the house and so they were caught.') She said the situation was serious because when Hendrik appeared before the magistrate the first time he told him he never wanted to see him appear in Court again . . . now he has an added offence.

She blames other mothers who let the gangs use their homes as 'headquarters' and let them cook their food and sit in their yard day-in and day-out. She finds them utterly irresponsible. She said it was getting so bad a while ago in Western Township with the youths lolling about on the stoops and shops and then suddenly pouncing on people that she and six other mothers led a delegation to the Police Station and said these boys must be removed as the place was getting unsafe. The situation had improved since the police had been around: 'But the police have also got other work to do, they can't just come all the time.'

Causes of gangsterism

When I asked her what she thought was the cause of Hendrik becoming a gangster – she said: 'It's the father. If the father is an alcoholic, how does he know how to talk to his son? How can he set an example in the house?' She sometimes tells her husband when he swears and shouts at Hendrik: 'That is not how you talk to a child and bring him up with respect.' She feels her sons have never had any guidance or discipline from their father, nor has he ever talked about anything with them. It is an awful experience for a son to come home and see his father performing because he is drunk. The father has even hit him in the past and she fears that one of these days Hendrik will have had enough and will beat up his father – because their relationship has reached the stage where anything the father says irritates the son and vice-versa. They can't bear the sight of each other.

Betty is an objective person and says she can't blame Hendrik, but at the same time she does not denigrate her husband: she is aware of his weaknesses. Betty has immense inner strength and is able to accept people's faults.

Betty feels that another reason for her son going astray is their poverty. They have never had more than just enough money for food and shelter. They have never had anything to spare for clothes, and even for school she could only give them essentials. Then she says: 'The children keep seeing the people walking up and down the streets in their nice clothes and they want them too. So they join up with a gang.'

Yes, she thinks the gangs also steal, otherwise where would they get their nice clothes from? During one of my visits Betty gave Hendrik R10 and told him to go and buy himself a decent pullover as the weather was turning cold. He returned in the evening without a pullover because the ones he liked cost R18.

Her retarded daughter

Betty's daughter, Cynthia, is 16 years old. She gave birth to her at home and had 'a terrible birth and I was sick from it'. Cynthia is retarded. During the day she goes to the only Johannesburg institution for handicapped Coloured children, which is in the neighbouring township of Coronationville. 'When she was born she had like a huge blister of blood on her head, and the woman who did the delivery knew nothing. In the end my mother-in-law came and took the baby to Baragwanath Hospital where they cut open her head and drained out the blood. I think the blood came there from the pressure in delivery or because I bumped myself when I was pregnant.' The child was born and had epileptic fits. She took her regularly to the 'convulsions clinic' where they gave her tablets. Lately she has stopped having fits. At 4½ she still couldn't walk.

At first Betty used to feel sorry for the child and then she realised that she would not help her by pampering, so she let her go out to play and fight with the other children.

While she had this child, Betty was unable to work – Cynthia demanded too much attention.

Cynthia's presence in the house is now disturbing. She is in her teens and froths and dribbles at the mouth constantly. She can't speak except by some primordially long dragged-out screeches, screams and hand-movements. Betty finds she is reaching a stage where she can't tolerate her any more. She becomes unbearable in that overcrowded two and a half-roomed house. Cynthia was attending the Coronation Day Care Centre but suddenly has refused to go. Apparently a child hit her at school so she won't go back. In addition to this she believes that only *'mal mense'* ('mad people') go there and she is not mad so she won't go to that school again!

She is also very dirty ('like a child') and Betty is at her wits end because the daughter is refusing to wash herself. She is becoming increasingly difficult to live with because some days she has terrible tempers and refuses to do anything and shouts and gets uncontrollably cross if the mother asks her to sweep the house or wash the dishes; on other occasions she is placid and no trouble. Betty feels she just can't have her about the house like this all day. But then she observes sweetly that she is learning to read nicely at school and even does little play acts for her mother.

Betty wants to have Cynthia sterilised at the hospital: 'They gave them birth-control injections at school, but I'm worried because Cynthia hasn't had her periods for three months. I will go to the hospital and ask for sterilisation.'

Betty's husband

Betty's own husband – 'his only fault is that he is an alcoholic'. He was once in hospital for TB, then he went back to work and now he's back in the TB hospital again and only recently returned home. *'Maar nou is hy gedaan, hy sal nie weer kan werk nie. Toe ek hom gister gesien het, het ek vir hom gesê, man, nou is jy gedaan.'* ('But now he's had it, he won't work again. When I saw him yesterday, I said to him, man, now you're finished.')

He gets a small Government pension of R29 a month off which they live. He first worked at a box manufacturing company. He liked work and worked hard, but after he had been to the TB hospital they wouldn't take him back again so he had to find other work. 'But now he's had it. He always used to give me his wages, he's a good man in that respect, but he used to like his bit of pocket money for himself. But he's an alcoholic . . . He won't go to SANCA or for treatment. He says there's nothing to live for, and that he had a friend who went to SANCA and during his treatment he got really ill; so he feels they wouldn't make him any better. I think he became an alcoholic just from habit. He has always drunk, but never so much; now he can't stop. He drinks wine, malmsey, and things like that, also BB [Bantu Beer] not brandy – that makes him sick. I drink just on weekends or when visiting friends. Usually he's very quiet, he hardly says two words to me, *maar as hy drink, kan hy vloek!* ('but when he drinks, can he swear!') He swears about everything and shouts and talks . . . Last night when he was shouting one of the twins came to the room and lifted his hand as though to smack him and walked out again.

'I always tell my husband that he does not know how to talk to the children, you still have to show them respect even if they are children. Otherwise they will just go their own way. And I tell my son-in-law that he must not drink so much, otherwise he will be the same as my husband.'

Betty finds that with her husband, his drinking and the difficult life she has had, her greatest strength '*dank die Here, is geduld*' ('thank the Lord, is patience.') When her daughter becomes furious with her husband about his drinking and wants to find somebody else, Betty tells her 'she must be patient and try to make a go of it with the husband she's got, she mustn't just go from man to man'.

Despite his drinking Betty has always supported her own husband morally, and says that although she is poor she has always 'had a roof over my head and some food to eat. Not like those people further down the road on the fields next to the shops where they sleep out in the veld because they have spent all their money on the shebeens and don't have any left for a home.'

Betty feels that the people prefer the shebeens to the official beer-halls and lounges (of which there are two in the neighbouring area of Newclare) because they have a more amenable atmosphere and stay open through the night, 'but it's at the shebeens that the trouble starts'.

We were once discussing the need for a disabled or old-age club film, or crafts or outings for the retired, which both Betty and her husband thought would be a very good idea, because they agreed he gets bored just sitting around all day. Betty also feels this is one of the reasons why he drinks.

When I inquired whether there was a council in the Township which could organise something on these lines, I got the stock reply – not to their knowledge. Betty then recalled: *'Ons hoor dat Y is 'n committee mens but ons sien hom nie . . . Oh ja ons het ook van 'n mens Z gehoor – maar hy het niks vir ons gedoen nie. Ek dink hulle praat net.'* ('We hear that Y is a committee man but we don't see him . . . Oh yes, and I also heard of a man Z – but he hasn't done anything for us. I think they just talk.')

Coming to terms with life

Betty feels that had they not been so poor, and had she had the opportunity, she could have gone far in school because she loves learning and reading. Even now her husband sometimes gets cross with her because she gets utterly lost in a book and she's in another world for a few hours and does not do a thing. She loves reading James Hadley Chase. She used to get library books, but they don't always have the books you want, or you don't always have the time to go down there, for there is much to do in the house. So when she can she buys her own paperback.

She has been a garment worker for many years and has worked all her life and has told her other daughter Eunice that if she doesn't go back to work now, then she must take the children back, and Betty will return: 'I am not afraid of work.' But she just had to buy spectacles for her eyes are not so good any longer.

Betty admits that she doesn't like living in Western Township, and if as rumour has it they will open Coronation dwellings for pensioners she will put their name on the list.

One day Betty visited a friend and genuinely admired her beautiful wall-to-wall carpet. She asked her what it cost. The reply was R300 and they were paying R20 a month hire purchase. 'I came home to my bare floor and decided I would rather live with peace and a bare floor.'

This little-educated but wise woman says she gets angry quickly, but once she has vented her anger all is forgiven and she carries on as before. Her neighbour once or twice made her cross and Betty wanted to tell her what she thought of her, but five minutes later she was back chatting with her over the fence again.

The last time I visited this family, in 1975, Betty at 50 was back at work. Her husband was making tea and Eunice was cleaning the house. Mr Snyman said they were relieved that their son Hendrik had been sent to a Cape Reformatory where he would learn a trade. Sadly he shook his head: *'Ek weet nie wat met die jong mense aangaan en wat met die Kleurlinge vandag gebeur. Ons het nie so gelewe nie.'* ('I don't know what is going on with the young people and what is happening to the Coloureds today. We didn't live like this.')

The house was choking with all Eunice's furniture and cement bags. She and her husband had been forced to move out of the flat where they were lodging to make room for a domestic servant. The 'Council' had promised them a flat for July 1974 but now had withdrawn the promise. So here they all were together with an electric stove, packed into a house which had no electricity and buying cement to try to add on a room.

I left this house sadly remembering the words her untutored mother had told me with a wink in a brighter moment: 'Well, after all, what did the poet say? All the world's a stage, and all the people, we are only players – oh, until the curtain goes down.'

Bibliography

Books marked with an asterisk have been particularly useful:

*Abramson, J. H. & Gampel, B. 1960 *Observations on the Nutritional State of Low-paid African Labourers in Natal* South African Medical Journal Vol 34 No. 50 pp. 1050-1057

Adams, G. 1974 *Armoede en die Kleurling* Social Work Vol 10 No 3 pp. 147, 177-184

*Aston, P. J. & Dobson, G. 1972 *Family Interaction and Social Adjustment in a Sample of Normal School Children* Journal of Child Psychology and Psychiatry Vol 13 No 2 pp. 77-89

Bakwin, H. 1942 *Loneliness in Infants* American Journal of Diseases of Children Vol 63 pp. 30-40

*Bales, R. F. 1946 *Cultural Differences in Rates of Alcoholism* Quarterly Journal of Studies on Alcohol Vol 6 pp. 480-499

*Batson, E. 1941 *Sub-Standard Living: Its Physical, Mental and Social Effects* Education Vol 51 No 8 pp. 111-119

Batson, E. 1942 *Contribution to the Study of Urban Coloured Poverty* South African Institute of Race Relations Journal Vol 9 pp. 2-11

*Becker, W. C. & Krug, R. S. 1965 *The Parent Attitude Research Instrument: A Research Review* Child Development Vol 36 No 2 pp. 329-365

Behrens, M. L. 1954 *Child Rearing and the Character Structure of the Mother* Child Development Vol 25 No 3 pp. 225-238

Beinart, J. 1965 *The Popular Art of Africa* Johannesburg, Institute for the Study of Man in Africa

*Bell, E. H. 1961 *Social Foundations of Human Behaviour* New York, Harper and Row

*Bell, N. W. & Vogel, E. Z. 1963 *A Modern Introduction to the Family* Free Press of Glencoe

*Bernal, J. & Richards, M. P. M. 1970 *The Effects of Bottle and Breast Feeding on Infant Development* Journal of Psychosomatic Research Vol 14 pp. 247-252

*Bevan, E. J. (ed.) 1972 *Index to South African Periodicals* Vol 31 1971 City of Johannesburg Public Library

Birtchnell, J. 1971 *Early Parent Death, in Relation to Size and Constitution of Sibship, in Psychiatric Patients and General Population Controls* Acta Psychiatrica Scandinavica Vol 47 pp. 250-270

*Botha, M. C. 1953-1956 *Report of the Coloured Education Commission* Cape Provincial Administration

*Bovet, L. 1951 *Psychiatric Aspects of Juvenile Delinquency* Geneva, WHO Monograph Series No 1

*Bowlby, J. 1966 *Maternal Care and Mental Health* WHO Monograph Series, No 2 New York, Schocken Books

*Bowlby, J. & Fry, M. 1973 *Child Care and the Growth of Love* (abr. rev. edn.) Middlesex, Penguin

Breytenbach, C. & Barrow, B. 1970 *The Spirit of District Six* Johannesburg, Purnell

*Brock, J. F. & Rollo, M. 1949 *The Cape Coloured People, Their Pattern of Health and Disease* South African Medical Journal Vol 23 December pp. 1000-1010

Bryant, A. T. 1966 *Zulu Medicine and Medicine-Men* Cape Town, C. Struik

Calderwood, D. M. 1959 *Native Housing Policies and Problems* Municipal Affairs Feb. Vol 24 No 282 pp. 10-11, 27, 60; Mar. Vol 24 No 283 pp. 33, 35, 75; Apr. Vol 24 No 284 pp. 61, 63

*Cilliers, S. P. 1963 *The Coloureds of South Africa* Cape Town, Banier

*Cilliers, S. P. (ed.) 1964 *Weskaapland – 'n Sosio-ekonomiese Studie* Stellenbosch, Kosmo

*Cilliers, S. P. 1971 *Appeal to Reason* Stellenbosch, University Publishers

Clear, J. P. 1959 *Subsidized Housing for the Middle Income Group – I* Municipal Affairs Nov. pp. 51, 53, 55. Part II in Dec. pp. 21, 23
Clegg, A. B. 1967 *The Excitement of Writing* London, Chatto & Windus
*Clinard, M. B. 1964 *Sociology of Deviant Behaviour* New York, Holt Rinehart & Winston
*Coetzee, H. S. 1971 *Die Ontstaansgeskiedenis van die Suid-Afrikaanse Kleurlinge* in *Die Kleurlinge in Suid-Afrika* Van Tonder, A. (ed.) Johannesburg, Afrikaanse Studentebond
*Coetzee, J. H. 1971 *Die Kulturele Identiteit van die Kleurling en Kulturele Verskeidenhede binne die Kleurlingbevolking* in *Die Kleurlinge in Suid-Afrika* Van Tonder, A. (ed.) Johannesburg, Afrikaanse Studentebond.
C.P.C. & A.J. 1956 *Housing for Coloured People in Cape Town and its Environs* The Bluestocking Vol 24 No 1 pp. 20-24
*Criteria Committee, National Council on Alcoholism, New York 1972 *Criteria for the Diagnosis of Alcoholism* Annals of Internal Medicine Vol 77 pp. 249-258
*Davis, D. R. 1971 *Interact and Communicate* British Journal of Disorders of Communication Vol 6 Apr. pp. 3-12
*Davis, K. 1966 *Human Society* New York, Collier-Macmillan
Dean, S. R. 1970-71 *Self-help Group Psychotherapy: Mental Patients Rediscover Will-Power* International Journal of Social Psychiatry Vol 42 No 1 pp. 72-78
*De Elejalde, F. 1971 *Inadequate Mothering; Patterns and Treatment* Bulletin of the Menninger Clinic Vol 35 No 3 pp. 182-198
*Department of Coloured Affairs 1954 *Consolidated General Bibliography, The Coloured People of South Africa* Cape Town Information Service
*Department of Coloured Affairs 1955 *General Bibliography, The Coloured People of South Africa* Suppl. No I Cape Town Information Service
Dickie-Clark, H. F. 1964 *The Marginal Situation; A Sociological Study of a Coloured Group* Thesis University of Natal
Du Plessis, I. D. 1972 *The Cape Malays* Cape Town A. A. Balkema
*Edelstein, M. L. 1973 *A Sociological Study of the Coloured Community of Johannesburg with Special Reference to Attitude Analysis* Thesis University of Pretoria
Edwards, G. 1973 *Epidemiology Applied to Alcoholism: A Review and an Examination of Purposes* Quarterly Journal of Studies on Alcohol Vol 34 pp. 28-56
*Eichinger Ferro-Luzzi, G. 1974 *Food Avoidances during the Puerperium and Lactation in Tamilnad* Ecology of Food and Nutrition Vol 3 No 1 pp. 7-15
*Erikson, E. H. 1972 *Childhood and Society* Middlesex Pelican
Federal Bureau of Investigation [F.B.I.] 1960 *Uniform Crime Reports* Annual Bulletin Washington D.C. Government Printing Office
[N.A.] 1958 *Financing of Municipal Housing with Special Reference to the Coloured Population* The South African Treasurer Vol 30 No 6 pp. 88, 90, 96
Fine, H. 1973 *A Brief Study of Juvenile Delinquency among the African and Coloured Communities with Particular Reference to the Johannesburg Magisterial District* Johannesburg South African Institute of Race Relations RR. 119/73
Forbes, C. 1973 *Rural Community Health* International Review of Mission Vol 62 No 246 pp. 212-215
*Forssman, H. & Thuwe, I. 1966 *One Hundred and Twenty Children Born After Application for Therapeutic Abortion Refused* Acta Psychiatrica Scandinavica Vol 42 pp. 71-88
Franco, S. C. 1954 *Problem Drinking and Industry: Policies and Procedures* Quarterly Journal of Studies on Alcohol Vol 15 pp. 453-468
Freud, S. 1948 *Collected Papers, Vol 2* London Hogarth Press and the Institute of Psycho-Analysis
*Gavron, H. 1970 *The Captive Wife: Conflicts of Housebound Mothers* Middlesex Penguin
Geach, H. 1973 *The Baby Food Tragedy* New Internationalist No 6 pp. 8-12, 23 & Editorial
Gillis, L. S. Lewis, J. & Slabbert, M. 1968 *Psychiatric Disorder Amongst the Coloured People of the Cape Peninsula* The British Journal of Psychiatry Vol 114 No 517 pp. 1575-1587

*Gillis, L. S. Lewis, J. & Slabbert, M. 1973 *Alcoholism Among the Cape Coloureds* South African Medical Journal Vol 47 No 30 pp. 1374-1382

*Glad, D. D. 1947 *Attitudes and Experiences of American-Jewish and American-Irish Male Youth as Related to Differences in Adult Rates of Inebriety* Quarterly Journal of Studies on Alcohol Vol 8 pp. 406-472

Graham, G. G. 1972 *Environmental Factors Affecting the Growth of Children* The American Journal of Clinical Nutrition Vol 25 pp. 1184-1188

*Gurland, B. J. Yorkston, N. J. Stone, A. R. Frank, J. D. & Fleiss, J. L. 1972 *The Structured and Scaled Interview to Assess Maladjustment* (SSIAM) Archives of General Psychiatry Vol 27 No 2 pp. 259-267

*György, P. & Kline, O. L. (eds.) 1970 *Malnutrition is a Problem of Ecology* Basel S. Karger

*Haer, J. L. 1955 *Drinking Patterns and the Influence of Friends and Family* Quarterly Journal of Studies on Alcohol Vol 16 pp. 178-185

*Harris, J. 1970 *The Working Mother: The Effect upon Home and Family* The Royal Society of Health Journal Vol 90 No 5 pp. 264-266, 284

Helm, B. 1950 *The Family Budgets of the Coloured People* South African Institute of Race Relations Journal Vol 17 pp. 15-21

*Hepner, R. & Maiden, N. C. 1971 *Growth Rate, Nutrient Intake and "Mothering" as Determinants of Malnutrition in Disadvantaged Children* Nutrition Reviews Vol 29 No 10 pp. 219-223

*Herzberg, F. 1966 *Work and the Nature of Man* New York, The World Publishing Company

Heymann, S. 1935 *Some Remarks on Infant-Feeding* South African Medical Journal Vol 9 No 11 pp. 377-381

Hinkle, L. E. Christenson, W. N. Kane, F. D. Ostfeld, A. Thetford, W. N. & Wolff, H. G. 1958 *An Investigation of the Relation Between Life Experience, Personality Characteristics and General Susceptibility to Illness* Psychosomatic Medicine Vol 20 No 4 pp. 278-295

Hobart Houghton, D. 1964 *The South African Economy* Cape Town, Oxford University Press

Horrell, M. 1970 *The Education of the Coloured Community in South Africa 1652-1970* Johannesburg, South African Institute of Race Relations

Horrell, M. & Horner, D. 1974 *A Survey of Race Relations in South Africa* Johannesburg, South African Institute of Race Relations

*Horton, D. 1943 *The Functions of Alcohol in Primitive Societies: A Cross-Cultural Study* Quarterly Journal of Studies on Alcohol Vol 4 pp. 199-320

*Howell, M. C. 1973 *Employed Mothers and Their Families (I)* Pediatrics Vol 52 No 2 pp. 252-263

*Howell, M. C. 1973 *Effects of Maternal Employment on the Child (II)* Pediatrics Vol 52 No 3 pp. 327-343

*Hseuh, A. M. Hsu, S. C. Chow, L. P. & Chow, B. F. 1973 *Maternal Nutrition: A Positive Approach in Family Planning* Ecology of Food and Nutrition Vol 2 No 2 pp. 99-106

Huddleston, T. 1971 *Naught for your Comfort* Collins Fontana Books

Hutt, W. H. 1964 *The Economics of the Colour Bar* London Andre Deutsch

Jackson, D. A. 1972 *Personnel Management* Johannesburg South African Broadcasting Corporation

Jelliffe, D. B. 1972 *Commerciogenic Malnutrition?* Nutrition Reviews Vol 30 No 9 pp. 199-205

*Jelliffe, D. B. & Jelliffe, E. F. P. 1973 *Education of the Public for Successful Lactation: Psychosocial Considerations* Ecology of Food and Nutrition Vol 2 No 2 pp. 127-132

*Jennings, H. 1967 *Societies in the Making: A Study of Development and Redevelopment Within a County Borough* London Routledge and Kegan Paul

Johnston, C. M. & Deisher, R. W. 1973 *Contemporary Communal Child Rearing: A First Analysis* Pediatrics Vol 52 No 3 pp. 319-326

Kephart, W. M. 1954 *Drinking and Marital Disruption* Quarterly Journal of Studies on Alcohol Vol 15 pp. 63-73

*Kerrin, J. 1945 *Drink and the Coloured Man* Trek Vol 9 No 18 p. 12
Kies, C. W. 1972 *Die Kleurlinge van Noord-Kaapland, Noord van die Oranjerivier* 2 Vols Thesis, University of Pretoria
King, M. H. King, F. M. A. Morley, D. C. Burgess, H. J. L. & Burgess, A. P. 1972 *Nutrition for Developing Countries: With Special Reference to the Maize, Cassava and Millet Areas of Africa* London, Oxford University Press
Lamont, A. McE. 1951 *Affective Types of Psychotic Reaction in Cape Coloured Persons* South African Medical Journal Vol 25 No 3 pp. 40-42
Landy, F. J. & Gaupp, L. A. 1971 *A Factor Analysis of the Fear Survey Schedule — III,* Behavioural Research and Therapy Vol 9 pp. 89-93
Larkin, F. A. 1971 *Pattern of Weaning in Dominica* West Indian Medical Journal Vol 20 No 3 pp. 229-236
Larsen, K. S. 1971 *Aggression — Altruism: A Scale and Some Data on its Reliability and Validity* Journal of Personality Assessment Vol 35 pp. 275-281
Lavis, S. W. 1938 *Some Adverse Social Conditions of the Coloured People and Their Effects* Cape Town Struik
*Lawler, E. E. 1970 *Job Design and Employee Motivation* in Vroom, V. H. & Deci, E. L. (eds.) *Management and Motivation* Middlesex Penguin Modern Management Readings
*Lewis, O. 1959 *Five Families, Mexican Case Studies in the Culture of Poverty* New York Basic Books
*Lidz, T. 1973 *Schizophrenia and the Family, the Origin and Treatment of Schizophrenic Disorders* New York Basic Books
Louw, E. F. 1974 *Alcoholism and the Employer — A Positive Policy* Rehabilitation in South Africa Vol 18 No 3 pp. 75-79
Luke, F. R. 1945 *The Economic Factor in Disease* Trek Vol 9 No 20 p. 13
*Lynd, R. S. & Lynd, H. M. 1929 *Middletown, A Study in American Culture* London Constable
*Maasdorp, G. & Humphreys, A. S. B. (eds.) 1975 *From Shantytown to Township; An Economic Study of African Poverty and Rehousing in a South African City* Cape Town Juta
Malinowski, B. 1968 *The Sexual Life of Savages in North-Western Melanesia* London Routledge & Kegan Paul
Mann, J. W. 1957 *The Problem of the Marginal Personality: A Psychological Study of a Coloured Group* Thesis University of Natal
Manuel, G. & Hatfield, D. 1967 *District Six* Johannesburg Longmans
Marais, J. S. 1957 *The Cape Coloured People 1652-1937* Johannesburg Witwatersrand University Press
*Marsden, D. 1973 *Mothers Alone: Poverty and the Fatherless Family* (rev. edn.) Middlesex Penguin
McBride, A. B. 1973 *The Anger-Depression Guilt Go-Round* American Journal of Nursing Vol 73 No 6 pp. 1045-1049
*McCord, W. & McCord, J. 1960 *Origins of Alcoholism* London Tavistock
*Menaker, E. 1973 *The Social Matrix: Mother and Child* The Psychoanalytic Review Vol 60 No 1 pp. 45-58
Mendels, J. & Weinstein, N. 1972 *The Schedule of Recent Experiences: A Reliability Study* Psychosomatic Medicine Vol 34 No 6 pp. 527-531
*Mindlin, R. L. & Lobach, K. S. 1971 *Consistency and Change in Choice of Medical Care for Pre-School Children* Pediatrics Vol 48 No 3 pp. 426-432
Moodie, A. D. Keet, M. P. Evans, D.E. Wittmann, W. & Hansen, J. D. L. 1972 *Environmental Stress and the Underprivileged Child: Kwashiorkor in Perspective* Ecology of Food and Nutrition Vol 1 No 2 pp. 95-101
Moore, E. C. 1897 *The Social Value of the Saloon* American Journal of Sociology Vol 3 No 1 pp. 1-12
Mowrer, H. R. & Mowrer, E. R. 1945 *Ecological and Familial Factors Associated with Inebriety* Quarterly Journal of Studies on Alcohol Vol 6 pp. 36-44
Müller, A. L. 1968 *Minority Interests: The Political Economy of the Coloured and Indian Communities in South Africa* Johannesburg South African Institute of Race Relations

Muller, H. n.d. *The Role of the Coloured People in the Economic Pattern of the Republic of South Africa* Grahamstown University Publishers
Nasionale Buro vir Opvoedkundige en Maatskaplike Navorsing [N.B.O.M.N.] 1964 *Die Kleurling: Samevattende Gegewens* Pretoria Departement van Onderwys, Kuns en Wetenskap
Nel, P. A. Loubser, M. & Steenekamp, J. J. A. 1972 *Income and Expenditure Patterns of Non-White Urban Households: Johannesburg Survey (Multiple Coloured Households)* Unisa Bureau of Market Research.
*Newson, J. & Newson, E. 1972 *Patterns of Infant Care in an Urban Community* Middlesex Penguin Books
*Niehoff, A. & Meister, N. 1972 *The Cultural Characteristics of Breast-Feeding: A Survey* Journal of Tropical Pediatrics and Environmental Child Health Vol 18 No 1 pp. 16-20
Nilsson, A. Uddenberg, N. & Almgren, P. E. 1971 *Parental Relations and Identification in Women with Special Regard to Para-Natal Emotional Adjustment* Acta Psychiatrica Scandinavica Vol 47 No 1 pp. 57-81
Oakland, L. & Kane, R. L. 1973 *The Working Mother and Child Neglect on the Navajo Reservation* Pediatrics Vol 51 No 5 pp. 849-853
*Park, P. 1962 *Problem Drinking and Role Deviation: A Study in Incipient Alcoholism* in Pittman, D. J. & Snyder, C. R. (eds.) *Society, Culture and Drinking Patterns* London John Wiley
*Plant, J. S. 1963 *Family Living Space and Personality Development* in Bell, N. W. & Vogel, E. Z. *A Modern Introduction to the Family* Free Press of Glencoe
Pokorny, A. D. Byron, A. Miller, M. S. & Kaplan, H. K. 1972 *The Brief MAST: A Shortened Version of the Michigan Alcoholism Screening Test* The American Journal of Psychiatry Vol 129 No 3 pp. 342-345
*Polansky, N. A. 1968 *Childhood Level of Living Scale* Athens University of Georgia School of Social Work
Pollak, H. 1971 *Education for Progress* Johannesburg South African Institute of Race Relations
Pomeroy, R. & Torres, M. A. 1972 *Family Planning Practices of Low Income Women in Two Communities* American Journal of Public Health Vol 62 No 8 pp. 1123-1129
Potgieter, J. F. & Fellingham, S. A. 1967 *Assessment of Methods for Dietary Surveys* South African Medical Journal Vol 41 No 35 pp. 886-890
[N.A.] 1942 *Protests from the Cape Flats* The Forum Dec. p. 17
Queen, S. A. & Habenstein, R. W. 1967 *The Family in Various Cultures* (3rd edn.) New York J. B. Lippincott
Rädel, F. E. De Coning, C. & Feldmann-Laschin, G. R. 1963 *Income and Expenditure Patterns of Urban Bantu Households, South-Western Townships Johannesburg* Unisa Bureau of Market Research
Randall, P. & Burrow, P. C. 1968 *Johannesburg's Coloured Community, With Especial Reference to Riverlea* Johannesburg South African Institute of Race Relations
*Raphael, D. 1973 *The Role of Breast-Feeding in a Bottle-Oriented World* Ecology of Food and Nutrition Vol 2 No 2 pp. 121-126
*Reader, D. H. 1964 *Sociological Aspects of Alcoholism* Psychologia Afrikana Vol 10 pp. 197-205
Reddy, S. K. 1971 *Artificial Feeding in Jamaica and Barbados* West Indian Medical Journal Vol 20 No 3 pp. 198-212
*Rip, C. M. 1964 *Group Affiliation and Participation and the Alcoholic* Thesis University of South Africa
Robertson, I. & Kemp, M. 1963 *Child Health and Family Size: A Survey Relating to the Cape Coloured Population of Cape Town in the Years 1961-2* South African Medical Journal Vol 37 No 35 pp. 888-893
Robinson, G. C. 1945 *Proper Attention to the Role of Emotional and Social Factors in Illness as a New Step in Public Health* The Milbank Memorial Fund Quarterly Vol 23 No 1 pp. 20-27
Roghmann, K. J. & Haggerty, R. J. 1970 *Rochester Child Health Surveys I: Objectives, Organisation and Methods* Medical Care Vol 8 No 1 pp. 47-59

Roghmann, K. J. & Haggerty, R. J. 1973 *Daily Stress, Illness and Use of Health Services in Young Families* Pediatric Research Vol 7 No 5 pp. 520-526

Rutter, M. 1973 *Maternal Deprivation Reassessed* Middlesex Penguin Education

*Salter Ainsworth, M. D. 1973 *Further Research into the Adverse Effects of Maternal Deprivation* in Bowlby, J. & Fry, M. (abr. edn.) *Child Care and the Growth of Love* (2nd edn.) Middlesex Penguin

Samson, E. 1971 *Beware! Anxious Mother at Work* British Dental Journal Vol 130 pp. 257-258

*Schaefer, E. S. & Bell, R. Q. 1958 *Development of a Parental Attitude Research Instrument (PARI)* Child Development Vol 29 No 3 pp. 339-361

Sibane, N. 1962 *Alcohol, the Friend of Crime* Our Africa, Sep. pp. 8, 15

Sibane, N. 1963 *He Doesn't Use a Gun — The Silent Killer Marches On* Our Africa Mar. pp. 8, 17

*Sims, L. S. Paolucci, B. & Morris, P. M. 1972 *A Theoretical Model for the Study of Nutritional Status: An Ecosystem Approach* Ecology of Food and Nutrition Vol 1 No 3 pp. 197-205

Smit, H. B. 1971 *Die Kleurlinge van Eesterrust se siening van hul huidige en toekomstige posisie in die breë Suid-Afrikaanse bevolkingstruktuur* Thesis University of Pretoria

Staples, R. & Smith, J. W. 1954 *Attitudes of Grandmothers and Mothers Toward Child Rearing Practices* Child Development Vol 25 No 2 pp. 91-97

Stone, F. H. 1971 *Psychological Aspects of Early Mother-Infant Relationships* British Medical Journal Vol 4 Oct. pp. 224-226

*Sub-Department of Coloured Affairs 1956 *The Coloured People of South Africa* Supplem. No 2 (General Bibliography)

[N.A.] *The Cape Coloured People Today* Johannesburg, South African Institute of Race Relations

Theron, E. 1955 *Die Kleurling en sy Maatskaplike Probleme* Pretoria, Van Schaik

Theron, E. (ed.) & Swart, M. J. 1964 *Die Kleurlingbevolking van Suid-Afrika* Stellenbosch, Universiteits Uitgewers

Tokar, J. T. Brunse, A. J. Stefflre, V. J. Napior, D. A. & Sodergren, J. A. 1973 *Emotional States and Behavioral Patterns in Alcoholics and Non-Alcoholics* Quarterly Journal of Studies on Alcohol Vol 34 pp. 133-143

Townsend, P. K. Liao, S. C. & Konlande, J. E. 1973 *Nutritive Contributions of Sago Ash Used as a Native Salt in Papua New Guinea* Ecology of Food and Nutrition Vol 2 No 2 pp. 91-97

Uddenberg, N. Almgren, P.-E. & Nilsson, A. 1971 *Birth Order and Sex of Siblings: Influence on Parental Identification* Acta Psychiatrica Scandinavica Vol 47 No 3 pp. 324-333

*Ullman, A. D. 1958 *Sociocultural Backgrounds of Alcoholism* The Annals of the American Academy of Political and Social Science Vol 315 Jan. pp. 48-54

Vahlquist, B. Stapleton, T. & Béhar, M. 1972 *New Urban Families* Acta Paediatrica Scandinavica Vol 61 No. 2 pp. 226-229

Van der Horst, S. T. n.d. *Poverty in Perspective* Topical Talks No. 6 Johannesburg South African Institute of Race Relations

*Van der Merwe, H. W. 1957 *Social Stratification in a Cape Coloured Community* Thesis, University of Stellenbosch

*Van der Merwe, R. 1974 *The Cost of Labour Turnover* People and Profits Vol 2 No 4 pp. 35-39

Van der Ross, R. E. 1971 *Deprivation among the Coloureds* New Nation Nov. pp. 9-14

*Van Tonder, A. (ed.) 1971 *Die Kleurlinge in Suid-Afrika* Johannesburg, Afrikaanse Studentebond

Van der Walt, T. 1970 *Huweliksverbintenisse tussen Kleurlingvroue en Bantoemans: 'n Sosiologiese ontleding van die huwelike van tweehonderd Kleurlingvroue met Bantoemans, woonagtig in die Kaapse Skiereiland* Thesis, University of Pretoria

*Vroom, V. H. & Deci, E. L. 1970 *Management and Motivation* Middlesex, Penguin Modern Management Readings

*Wallace, H. M. & Gold, E. M. 1972 *The Relationship of Family Planning to Pediatrics and Child Health* Journal of Tropical Pediatrics and Environmental Health Vol 18 No 1 pp. 8-10

Walther, M. (Brindley) 1968 *Patterns of Life in Domestic Service* Thesis University of the Witwatersrand

Watson, G. 1970 *Passing for White — A Study of Racial Assimilation in a South African School* London, Tavistock

*Wedge, P. & Prosser, H. 1973 *Born to Fail?* London, Arrow Books

Whalen, T. 1953 *Wives of Alcoholics: Four Types Observed in a Family Service Agency* Quarterly Journal for Studies on Alcohol Vol 14 No 4 pp. 632-641

Whisson, M. G. & Van der Merwe, H. W. (eds.) 1972 *Coloured Citizenship in South Africa* Cape Town, The Abe Bailey Institute of Inter-Racial Studies

Whisson, M. G. 1971 *The Coloured People* The Abe Bailey Institute of Inter-Racial Studies, Reprint No 5, University of Cape Town

Whisson, M.G. n.d. *The Fairest Cape? An Account of the Coloured People in the District of Simonstown* Johannesburg, South African Institute of Race Relations

Wittkower, E. D. 1948 *The Psychological Aspects of Venereal Disease* British Journal of Venereal Diseases Vol 24 pp. 59-67

Wright, L. 1971 *Comparison of Two Sociometric Devices for Measuring Personality Integration* Psychological Reports Vol 29 pp. 1035-1039

Wright, N. H. 1972 *Some Estimates of the Potential Reduction in the United States Infant Mortality Rate by Family Planning* American Journal of Public Health Vol 62 No 8 pp. 1130-1134

Wyatt, F. 1971 *A Clinical View of Parenthood* Bulletin of the Menninger Clinic Vol 35 No 3 pp. 167-181

Ziervogel, C. n.d. *Brown South Africa* Cape Town, Maskew Miller

Acknowledgements

I should like to express my gratitude to the following people and institutions: the School of Pathology, South African Institute for Medical Research, Professor J. Metz, and the University of the Witwatersrand for facilities in connection with the socio-medical research which preceded this study; Dr G. M. Margo with whom I undertook the original Nutritional research; and the Anglo-American Corporation of South Africa for sponsoring that work. With regard to the material in this book I should like to thank the Johannesburg City Council Coloured and Asian Division, Mr R. Stewart, and all the Governmental and Municipal Departments and Personnel connected with the Township who offered assistance, especially the City Health Division; SANCA and other professionals who discussed ideas with me; the Coloured men, women and children of Western Township for their help and friendship; and finally my husband who meticulously edited the manuscript: every thanks.

A copy of this manuscript has been forwarded to the Theron Commission of Inquiry into Matters Related to the Coloured Population Group in South Africa.

Index